This is an outstanding read on everything that goes into excellence. Ryan delivers real, practical, and profound insights into the pursuit of a standard of excellence in our lives and work. The anecdotes are fascinating and speak to his years of detailed study of high-achieving people, as well as his own pursuit of this standard. I thoroughly enjoyed reading it and look forward to more of Ryan's work.

— CHRIS HOLTMANN, Head Coach of the Ohio State University Men's Basketball Team

Ryan Hawk has led teams on the football field, in the boardroom, and while working with senior leaders in corporate America. He's learned how to build trust, take action, and get results. If you want to do the same, read this book!

— JOEL PETERSON, Chairman of JetBlue Airways and author of *The 10 Laws of Trust*

Ryan Hawk conducted one of the most thoughtful interviews I've ever had. He probed for ideas that are down to earth and practical for all.

— JEFF IMMELT, former CEO of GE and author of *Hot Seat*

Ryan Hawk is a master of dualities: He's a great leader, but also a ferocious learner. He's an accomplished athlete, but he has also excelled in the business world. He's eminently interesting, but he's also genuinely interested. Ryan has uncovered the secrets of what the best leaders do and how they think. Do yourself and your team a favor and read this book.

— LIZ WISEMAN, *New York Times* bestselling author of *Multipliers* and *Rookie Smarts*

Ryan Hawk is someone who points the way, illustrating how you can't lead a team or a company until you first learn to lead yourself. He offers inspiring and practical advice based on his lessons as a sports and business athlete and shares insights he's learned from others along the way.

— BETH COMSTOCK, former Vice Chair of GE and bestselling author of *Imagine It Forward*

Ryan Hawk is that rarest of people—a truly curious soul who asks questions that drill down into the heart of the matter, leave space for contemplation, and gently urge his subjects to look inside for answers they might not yet have discovered themselves.

—ROBERT KURSON, *New York Times* bestselling author of *Shadow Divers*

From the time he was a young high school and collegiate quarterback to the present, Ryan Hawk has always had the passion to serve and to lead. His presentations, podcasts, and books will make a difference in many lives.

—JIM TRESSEL, President of Youngstown State University and former Coach of the National Champion Ohio State University Football Team

THE PURSUIT OF EXCELLENCE

THE PURSUIT OF EXCELLENCE

THE UNCOMMON BEHAVIORS OF
THE WORLD'S MOST PRODUCTIVE ACHIEVERS

RYAN HAWK

Mc
Graw
Hill

New York   Chicago   San Francisco   Athens   London   Madrid
Mexico City   Milan   New Delhi   Singapore   Sydney   Toronto

1 2 3 4 5 6 7 8 9   LCR   26 25 24 23 22 21

ISBN   978-1-264-26909-9
MHID   1-264-26909-9

e-ISBN   978-1-264-26910-5
e-MHID   1-264-26910-2

Library of Congress Cataloging-in-Publication Data

Names: Hawk, Ryan, author.
Title: The pursuit of excellence : the uncommon behaviors of the world's most productive
    achievers / Ryan Hawk.
Description: New York : McGraw Hill, [2021] | Includes bibliographical references and index.
Identifiers: LCCN 2021037307 (print) | LCCN 2021037308 (ebook) | ISBN 9781264269099
    (hardback) | ISBN 9781264269105 (ebook)
Subjects: LCSH: Success. | Excellence. | Success in business. | Leadership.
Classification: LCC BF637.S8 H336 2021 (print) | LCC BF637.S8 (ebook) | DDC 158—dc23
LC record available at https://lccn.loc.gov/2021037307
LC ebook record available at https://lccn.loc.gov/2021037308

McGraw Hill books are available at special quantity discounts to use as premiums and sales promotions or for use in corporate training programs. To contact a representative, please visit the Contact Us pages at www.mhprofessional.com.

McGraw Hill is committed to making our products accessible to all learners. To learn more about the available support and accommodations we offer, please contact us at accessibility@ mheducation.com. We also participate in the Access Text Network (www.accesstext.org), and ATN members may submit requests through ATN.

To my grandpa Dean Hawk—

thank you for showing me what it means to be a leader

CONTENTS

PART I

THE BUILD

PART II

THE FUEL

PART III

THE CHASE

FOREWORD

If you have only recently come to learn about Ryan Hawk, I suppose you could go listen to the over 400 interviews Ryan has generated for his award-winning podcast, *The Learning Leader Show*—and I'd recommend that. Another way to catch the spirit of the podcast is to read this book. In it, Ryan has distilled the wisdom he's learned from two sources: seven years of interviewing some of the best leaders in the world and thousands of hours of study and practice in his own life.

When I first met Ryan on *The Learning Leader Show*, I was certain I had stumbled upon one of the most impressive leaders and teachers of leaders in the world. He doesn't come from New York City or Washington, D.C., or Silicon Valley. Ryan's from Dayton, Ohio, and he isn't enamored with title or status. He just wants all of us to be better, and he does that by giving us access to real-world, humble leaders who are in the trenches with their people—those who have learned how to lead through trial and error.

Ryan Hawk certainly didn't know what his podcast would become when he posted his first episode seven years ago. Or maybe he did; he's that kind of guy. But he couldn't have anticipated that he would bring so many people together to share their experiences in such a powerful way.

This book is the culmination of that adventure in learning and teaching. Ryan has systematically observed the world's most excellent leaders, and then assembled those observations into a toolkit, outlining the actions and attitudes that drive achievement. This book is an absolute must-read if you care to live an excellent life.

Having spent hours with Ryan on- and off-air, I'm inspired by his dedication to producing excellent work and pursuing excellence in his own life—all with an eye to serving the community he's worked so hard to build. Take the time to read this book and ask yourself how these words can make you a better leader and a better person right now.

Thank you, Ryan, for bringing us this gem: *The Pursuit of Excellence.*

PATRICK LENCIONI
Founder and CEO of The Table Group
Bestselling author of *The Five Dysfunctions of a Team*
and *The Advantage*

INTRODUCTION

When not crashing their flying machine prototype into the sand dunes of Kitty Hawk, North Carolina, Orville and Wilbur Wright spent large swaths of time sitting on the beach watching birds and imitating their movements. At least, that is how it appeared to the locals who took notice. "We couldn't help thinking they were just a pair of poor nuts," recounted Kitty Hawk resident John T. Daniels. "They'd stand on the beach for hours at a time, just looking at the gulls flying, soaring, dipping. They would watch the gannets and imitate the movements of their wings with their arms and hands. They could imitate every movement of those gannets; we thought they were crazy, but we just had to admire the way they could move their arms this way and that and bend their elbows and wrist bones up and down and which way, just like the gannets."[1]

But what looked like a weird habit was actually Orville and Wilbur studying how to fly. What better model than birds? Wilbur filled pages of his notebook with drawings and observations about the differences among how buzzards, eagles, and hawks rode the air. "The buzzard," he wrote, "which uses the dihedral angle finds greater difficulty to maintain equilibrium in strong winds than eagles or hawks which hold their wings level. The hen hawk can rise faster than the buzzard and its motion is steadier. It displays less effort in maintaining its balance. Hawks are better soarers than the buzzards but more often resort to flapping because they wish greater speed. A damp day is unfavorable for soaring unless there is a high wind. No bird soars in a calm."[2] In the margins next to his observations, Wilbur drew the different birds and their wing angles. He paid close attention to the subtle

1

differences in wing inclination, center of gravity, and the "fore-and-aft equilibrium" that all factored into lift and flight. Orville explained it succinctly: "Learning the secret of flight from a bird was a good deal like learning the secret of magic from a magician."[3]

In Dayton, Ohio, I grew up with the legacy of the Wright Brothers. The fingerprints of civic pride in the turn-of-the-century Daytonians who unlocked the secret of powered human flight are everywhere. There is the series of national aviation history museum sites on Dayton's west side: The Wright Brothers' family home and their bicycle shop, the places where their dreams and theories about flight took shape. The over 8,000 acres of Wright-Patterson Air Force Base (WPAFB) encompass the field on Dayton's east side where the brothers perfected their Wright Flyer after its historic first flight. Located next to WPAFB is Wright State University. Drive through the center of Dayton's downtown and you will pass under a gorgeous piece of abstract art known as "Flyover" that traces the 150-foot-long and 43-foot-high flight path of the Wright Brothers' first flight.

Over the years, a methodology has emerged that drives my pursuit of excellence following this very same pattern. Just as the Wright Brothers were fascinated by the movements of birds, I am fascinated by the stories behind personal and organizational excellence. Just as they took note of the most fundamental details of how birds moved their bodies to harness the forces of lift, I love distilling the examples of excellence in others down to their component parts. My goal is to understand why it happened. Was it intentional, deliberate action that caused the outcome, or was it luck? How did that result come about? What was the series of events that led to it? When I can identify the actions, behaviors, habits, routines, and rituals of those who sustain excellence, I implement them to see what works for me and what could work for others. This approach and that effort have culminated in the book you are now holding.

SUCCESS VERSUS EXCELLENCE

What's the difference between success and excellence? It's a question I hear often, and it's one I have asked myself and others many times. The person whose answer I find myself sharing with others the most is that of a high school basketball coach named Brook Cupps. Brook is the head basketball coach at my alma mater, Centerville High School. He coached the elite-level AAU team that featured both his own son, Gabe, and the son of LeBron James, LeBron James Jr. In 2021, he led Centerville to its first-ever state championship (Gabe was the leading scorer in the championship game).

Over the past few years, Brook has become one of my most valued friends because he embodies what it means to live true to your values. I have long been an admirer of how he does more than just teach basketball to the young people in his charge. He instills in them the lessons of leadership and, specifically, a thirst for excellence. When I asked Brook what the difference is between success and excellence, he replied, "Success is based on a comparison with others. Excellence is measured against your own potential."

His answer is so simple, yet so true. The only comparison I should be making is with myself. Will I be better tomorrow than I am today? Will I be more thoughtful, more intentional, more purposeful in the future than I am right now? Do my habits, routines, rituals, and actions match my intention to be better tomorrow than I am today? These questions are the gateway to excellence because living a life of excellence is about the fanatical pursuit of gradual improvement. I like the way author Darren Hardy describes the compounding effect of gradual improvement: "It's the principle of reaping huge rewards from a series of small, smart choices. Small, Smart Choices + Consistency + Time = RADICAL DIFFERENCE."[4]

DON'T SACRIFICE THE GIFT

Why not be satisfied with the attainable goal of "success" rather than opting for the hard road of continuous but never finished "improvement"? Why pursue excellence when winning can be had for less? The words of famed long-distance runner Steve Prefontaine accurately capture how I feel: "To give anything less than your best is to sacrifice the gift."

Steve Prefontaine set American records at every distance from 2,000 to 10,000 meters as he prepared for the 1976 Olympics. Known simply as "Pre" in the running world, he was renowned for setting an extraordinarily fast pace. He said, "A lot of people run a race to see who is fastest. I run to see who has the most guts, who can punish himself into an exhausting pace, and then at the end, punish himself more."[5]

This is a different way of viewing what a race is all about: as a test of yourself, not a means of comparing yourself to others. Can you be better this time than you were last time? What are you doing to intentionally improve yourself? That's what excellence is about. The primary comparison you should get in the habit of making is the one with your previous self. What are you doing to be better tomorrow than you are today? Who are you surrounding yourself with to ensure that? What habits are you creating to consistently improve over time? All these actions and thoughts come from intention and living with purpose. I won't say that this is the easiest way to live, but I think it's the most fulfilling.

Always striving to do better is a challenge. I'm driven to meet that challenge. To not pursue excellence would feel like I'm wasting this wonderful opportunity I've been given. The pursuit of excellence is about maximizing my potential. The chase is about not just accepting the problems and struggles that are inevitable parts of life. It is about embracing them. Why not aggressively attack them?

I'm fueled by feedback that what I do helps people. I'm motivated by positively impacting the lives of others, whether friends or complete strangers. I relish the challenge of helping high performers—people who are smarter than me, have already accomplished a lot, and have the titles to prove it. Accepting that challenge means showing up and doing it well. But embracing that challenge also means daring them to do the same and pushing them to aim higher.

I feel a sense of responsibility to be excellent based on the fortunate circumstances into which I am grateful to have been born. As I've gotten older, I've realized just how fortunate I am to have been nurtured throughout my life by my parents, my brothers, my coaches, and great bosses. I wonder what I have done to deserve that.

And yet, here I am with many people who believe in me. I love proving those people right. That's why I am committed to pursuing excellence. If I'm always trying to get better and that effort shows up in the results of my work, then I'm bound to be useful to others. If my work helps them, then that validates the investments in me of my supporters.

I can't imagine not living this way. I love the thought that my work moves people to take action in their lives. To do that, I can't be satisfied with the goal of being "great." I have to aim higher—for excellence. That is what I want my life to be all about.

THE PURSUIT

A pursuit is a chase or quest for something. It's a word that comes from the Anglo-French *purseute*, which means "the act of pursuing or striving toward goals."[6] Movement, action, effort, and exertion are all required elements of a pursuit. Author and leadership legend John Maxwell told me, "Action shows intention. Nobody ever wanted to follow me when I was sitting my butt in the sand. That's why I'm always moving."[7]

Pursuing excellence requires that same mindset—one that is biased toward action. It is the pursuit of getting better. It is not about the achievement of climbing a mountain. It is about climbing the next taller mountain. Without progress and growth, there is no life. Without endurance in the pursuit, there is no excellence. The pursuit of excellence is a form of what Simon Sinek calls an "infinite game": one where "there is no finish line, no practical end to the game . . . no such thing as 'winning' . . . [where] the primary objective is to keep playing, to perpetuate the game."[8] It is about pushing yourself beyond the edges of your zone of comfort and competency. Then once you adapt and establish a new horizon of what is comfortable, pushing yourself beyond it again. And again. And again.

WHY?

In my first book, *Welcome to Management*, I focused on a very specific moment in one's journey of leadership: the transition from working as an individual contributor to leading as a just-promoted, first-time manager. That book was intended to serve as a reference manual for the new leader, the kind of book bosses would give to people along with the news they were being promoted to a leadership position, the type of book a manager might turn to again and again over the next few years, as they navigate the new terrain of management responsibility.

With this book, *The Pursuit of Excellence*, my goal is to be both practical and aspirational: to dig into what excellence is, why it matters, and how to go about pursuing it. This book is for growth-oriented, hardworking people who think rigorously. It may not be for everyone.

I'm often asked by colleagues, friends, podcast listeners, and clients, "What are the common themes you find among the guests you speak with? What do they do?" This book is my answer. There are several distinct lessons I need to share, and my experiences interviewing people such as Jim Collins, Kat Cole, Dan Pink, Admiral William McRaven, Jeni Britton Bauer, George Raveling, Patrick Lencioni, Susan Cain, and hundreds of other high achievers help make that possible. Along with their invaluable insights, I draw on over two decades of my own learning by trial and error. I lay it all out on the table in both a descriptive and prescriptive manner. Over the course of this journey together, we will zoom out to the 30,000-feet view of what makes excellence and zoom in to street level to examine the tactics, behaviors, and actions taken by noted high performers across a wide variety of domains. As you read, you may encounter ideas that will invite you to question yourself and your beliefs. That's OK. It's part of the journey. You will also find specific actions to take, experiments to run, and tools to analyze what works best for you as you pursue your own brand of excellence. What should you continue to do, and what should you stop? Productive achievers live lives full of experiments, and I want to both inspire you and equip you to do just that.

PART I

THE BUILD

1

PURPOSE MINDSET

The key to pursuing excellence is to embrace an organic, long-term learning process, and not to live in a shell of static, safe mediocrity. Usually, growth comes at the expense of previous comfort or safety.
—JOSH WAITZKIN

For the first two and a half decades of my life, my passion and purpose were all about sports. I wanted to play football and planned to do that as my life's work. Through football, I was able to earn a full scholarship that paid for my college education (and room and board). But life sometimes has a funny way of letting you know that your plans aren't going to work out. While I was passionate about earning a living as a quarterback, the key decision makers determined that I was not good enough to play in the NFL. The universe retired me from my dream, and I was forced to figure out how to find my next passion.

With the help of a family friend, I landed a job in telephonic sales. It was a humbling moment. Did I grow up saying, "Wow, I hope I can get a job in a cubicle making 70 cold calls a day for a living?" Of course not. I haven't met anyone who has. But I know a lot of people who grow up wanting to do excellent work that fulfills them.

In a survey conducted by the Stanford Center on Longevity, 77 percent of Americans said they want to live to be at least 100 years old.[1] While a healthy diet full of whole foods and regular exercise increase our odds, there is one key element that science shows we often overlook: finding purpose.

According to the *Washington Post*, "Research reveals that people who believe their existence has meaning have lower levels of the stress hormone cortisol and more favorable gene expression related to inflammation. If a 90-year-old with a clear purpose in life develops Alzheimer's disease, that person will probably keep functioning relatively well despite real pathological changes in the brain, one study found. Another meta-analysis of 10 studies involving more than 136,000 people found that having purpose in life can lower your mortality risk by about 17 percent."[2] The simple fact is that any job in any profession can do this for anyone. Find your purpose and meaning in the job you have, and excellence becomes possible.

As I embarked on my new path as a telephonic sales rep, I learned that implementing a similar work ethic from my playing days to the world of professional selling would be helpful. I realized that my love for competition could still apply by competing against both my own prior performance and the performance of my peers. I discovered that I enjoyed helping my customers and that I got fulfillment out of helping my teammates and my manager. Did I love the actual job? Was it my passion? Not necessarily. But there were many elements of the work that I came to love.

Eventually, I became good at the job. I developed some mastery for how to do it well. I was given autonomy by my boss because of the results I produced for him and the company. I developed relationships with many coworkers who became my friends for life. I started looking forward to Monday mornings and the grind of each week. I loved that it was hard and that only a few of us could achieve the "Circle of Excellence" status that the company had established for the highest performers. I enjoyed the pursuit and the challenge to perform at higher levels. I felt fulfilled by improving my skills at something I had previously never done.

The passion came after the performance. I became passionate about the work because I developed a high level of skill to do it well.

And the same is true for what I do now for a living. I am immensely curious about understanding the frameworks of excellence of others. Because of that, I launched a podcast with the intent of creating a platform to enable me to have long-form conversations with fascinating people who have sustained excellence. That curiosity has driven me to work at the craft of asking thoughtful questions, developing better listening skills, and asking even better follow-up questions. My passion for this work has grown over the many years I've done it. Once I've developed a skill, it fuels my purpose and gives me more fulfillment. That drives me to work on it even more, which helps me get better over time.

The improvement of my output has opened countless doors for other career and relationship opportunities. The podcast has become the basis for my full-time work. I've built a business from it. I've created products and services such as my Learning Leader Circles, which are paid mastermind groups, or The Learning Leader Academy, my online school for leaders. I now regularly give keynote speeches for a wide variety of companies and conferences, and I work with the leadership teams of those companies to help them be more effective. All these opportunities have resulted from *The Learning Leader Show*, and that was born out of my choice to be purposeful about my work long before I uncovered a passion for it.

When asked for advice, Professor Scott Galloway said, "The worst advice given to young people is . . . follow your passion. If someone tells you to follow your passion, that means they're already rich. Your job is to find something you're good at. And then spend thousands of hours and apply the grit and the sacrifice and the willingness to break through hard things to become great at it. Because once you're great at something, the economic accoutrements of being great at something, the prestige, the relevance, the camaraderie, the self-worth of being great . . . will make you passionate about whatever it is. Here's the problem with believing you should follow your passion: Work is hard. And when you run into obstacles and you face injustice, which is a common guaranteed attribute of the workplace, you'll start thinking, 'I'm not loving this. This is upsetting and hard. It must not be my passion.' That is not the right litmus test. Jay-Z followed his passion and is a billionaire. Assume you are not Jay-Z ."[3]

This is the same advice I received years ago from Cal Newport, author of *So Good They Can't Ignore You* and *Deep Work*: " 'Follow your passion' is bad advice for a few reasons. The first is that most people don't have a clear predefined passion to follow. This is especially true if you consider young people who are just setting out on their own for the first time. The advice to follow your passion is frustratingly meaningless if, like many people, you don't have a passion to follow. The second reason is that we don't have much evidence that matching your job to a preexisting interest makes you more likely to find that work satisfying. The properties we know lead people to enjoy their work—such as autonomy, mastery, and relationships—have little to do with whether or not the work matches an established inclination."[4]

IT'S ABOUT GROWTH

Dr. Carol Dweck was born in New York in 1946, the middle child of three. In sixth grade, Carol and the rest of her fellow students were seated in order of their IQ. The children with the highest IQs in the class were the only ones entrusted with special classroom duties: washing the blackboard, carrying the flag, or taking a note to the principal's office for the teacher. Carol said, "On the one hand, I didn't believe that a score on a test was that important; on the other hand, every student wants to succeed in the framework that's established. So, looking back, I think that glorification of IQ was a pivotal point of my development."[5]

In fact, that experience set up the trajectory of her professional scholarship decades later. For her PhD, Dweck asked children to answer a series of increasingly harder questions. Her goal was to measure how they responded to questions they eventually would get wrong. She wanted to see how they would cope with it. "I was quite amazed when some of the kids got excited when I gave them problems they couldn't solve . . . my eyes kind of bugged out. Those kids taught me something that determined the rest of my career. I wanted to figure out what kind of 'special sauce' they had, and I wanted to bottle it—that is what I devoted my career to."[6]

Dr. Dweck would later publish her bestselling book, *Mindset: The New Psychology of Success*. In it, she lays out the differences between what she calls the fixed mindset (the belief that growth potential is limited by inherited traits like IQ) and the growth mindset (the belief that inherited traits merely provide the starting point for nearly limitless growth potential). Her research suggests that teachers can foster students' growth mindset by teaching them that intelligence can be developed, which helps them to embrace challenges and the rewards that come with hard work and effort, not just those that flow from their inherent intelligence. When I spoke with Dr. Dweck on my podcast, she shared her thoughts about the problems associated with having a fixed mindset, as well as tangible actions you can take—both as a parent raising a child and for managing yourself. Here are a few:

- ▶ Be aware that doing something the hard way will benefit you (and your children).
- ▶ Fixed mindset leaders have a deep-seated insecurity. "They have to keep showing that they're a genius."
- ▶ People with a fixed mindset are afraid to find out that they aren't very smart.
- ▶ Ask yourself, When was the last time I was wrong? (This is healthy. Do it often.)
- ▶ Sharing credit or taking it all for yourself? It shows a lot about your mindset. Growth mindset leaders share credit with others because nobody is self-made. We're all community made.
- ▶ Do not reward children for getting straight As. Instead, focus on their willingness to push themselves with classes outside of their comfort zone and the attitude they bring to the class. I learned from Carol to read the teacher's comments first and talk with my children about those comments before looking at the grades.

Give positive reinforcement to growth mindset characteristics like effort, attitude, and willingness to take on a challenge.
- ▶ "Don't praise intelligence. Praise the process."
- ▶ Don't declare that you have a growth mindset. Instead, figure out what triggers you into having a fixed mindset. Start there.[7]

Dr. Dweck asks readers of her work a series of pointed, thought-provoking questions that are critical guideposts for the pursuit of excellence. "Why waste time proving over and over how great you are, when you could be getting better? Why hide deficiencies instead of overcoming them? Why look for friends or partners who will just shore up your self-esteem instead of ones who will also challenge you to grow? And why seek out the tried and true, instead of experiences that will stretch you? The passion for stretching yourself and sticking to it, even (or especially) when it's not going well . . . this is the mindset that allows people to thrive during some of the most challenging times in their lives."[8]

SELF-AUDIT

On September 15, 2008, the financial system ground to a near-complete halt under the rising tide of subprime mortgage defaults. The chain reaction had been slow rolling across the economy since early that spring, when the investment bank Bear Stearns had to sell itself for cents on the dollar to avoid bankruptcy. On that fall morning, the collapsing housing market claimed its most shocking casualty. Lehman Brothers, the fourth-largest investment bank in the country, abruptly filed for the largest bankruptcy in US history. The death of this nearly 160-year-old firm suddenly threw its 25,000 global employees out of work and sent the stock market to its biggest single-day plunge since the terrorist attacks of 9/11.[9]

At the time, Ryan Serhant was a 24-year-old struggling actor and hand model starting his career as a real estate broker in New York City.

He was trying to learn the ropes of his new job while suddenly competing against 80,000 other real estate agents all struggling to even get rental listings. At this point, Ryan told me, he did what he calls a "self-audit." He went to his closest friends and colleagues and asked them one question: "When I'm not around and you're describing me to someone else, what do you say?" He explained, "How they describe you to others (when you're not around) is the real perception of you, your character, and your brand."[10]

What Ryan learned from this exercise was tough to hear. His peers described him as the guy who couldn't look someone in the eye, who would awkwardly put his hands in his pockets and regularly fail to muster the courage to talk to people. Ryan knew that in the real estate business, this image—his personal brand—was not going to work. After incorporating this information and implementing personal changes, the results ultimately spoke for themselves. Ryan's self-audit led to him becoming the leader of the number one real estate team in New York City, selling $1.45 billion worth of real estate in 2019.

In 2012, just four years after getting his start in the real estate world, Ryan went to an open audition to become a cast member for the Emmy-nominated television show *Million Dollar Listing New York*. He showed up along with 3,000 other real estate brokers. His chances seemed less than small. He didn't have the connections of a big New York family. He did not come from money. In fact, he was still learning his craft and had not sold much to that point.

"What did you say?" I asked him. "How did you get cast for that show?" He answered, "I sold them on the person that I was going to become, not the person I was at the moment." As anyone familiar with the show knows, his approach worked: Ryan is now one of its stars. He has gone on to have his own show, *Sell It Like Serhant*, and has published a book with the same title.[11]

The point of this story is Ryan's willingness to do regular audits of himself. He was unafraid to hold a mirror up and see its honest reflection. He asked his friends and colleagues to give a true assessment of what he brings to the table. Years later, watching Ryan on my podcast or on his TV show, one would never guess he was someone who lacked confidence or couldn't look you in the eye. He is the opposite of that now.

The idea of *becoming* is a through-point in this entire book. We must possess the mindset of putting in the necessary work to constantly improve and grow. In the process of getting cast on *Million Dollar Listing New York*, Ryan Serhant was asked for his one-line mantra. He thought, "I'm all about growth, all about getting bigger and leading an empire." So he said, "Expansion. Always, in all ways." It's memorable and true. It's what his friends say about him when he's not around.

What do your friends say about you when you're not around? How would they describe you in one sentence to others? Ask them. Learn. And then work to make that one-sentence description what you want it to be.

"THIS IS A PROCESS"

I love learning how world-class performers produce their work. What I find so fascinating is how unique the processes are that creators use to pursue their craft. Their methods are as diverse as their personalities. Take, for example, Billy Joel: the five-time Grammy Award–winning songwriter and musician who is not only a member of the Rock and Roll Hall of Fame but is also the *only* nonclassical musician to have his portrait on display in the midtown Manhattan showroom of the famous piano maker Steinway & Sons.[12]

Singer-songwriter Tom Bahler recounted a writing session he had with Billy Joel that turned into the hit song, "For the Longest Time." As Bahler recalls, Billy Joel came into the studio with "a spiral-bound college notebook." Bahler sees Joel turn to a blank page in the notebook, jot down the title "For the Longest Time," and start writing lyrics. After the Piano Man finished filling up the page with the new song's lyrics, he turned the page and wrote them all again. Only this time, Bahler noticed it was with the exception of the title. Joel simply rewrote the lyrics from start to finish, with only a word or two being different from the version on the preceding page.

According to Bahler, this repetitive process of evolution continued for "like 10 or 20 times" before Joel closed the notebook. The scene prompted Bahler to blurt out, "What the hell?"

"What?!" responded Joel.

"Well, Billy," said Bahler, "I'm a writer, and most writers—I don't know anybody who writes like that. If we get an idea, we cross out a line and replace it."

"Oh no, no, no, man. I don't do that," Joel said. "That would send my subconscious a message that I had made a mistake. And this is a process," he added, holding up the notebook. The message left a lasting impact on Bahler. He explains, "That's one of the most important lessons I've ever learned, and I'll never forget that moment."[13]

That story illustrates the intricacies and quirks of a process unique to one person. Billy Joel's process is what helps get the genius from his head to the page and ultimately to our ears. While it may not be the process for others, it's his. And that's what is most important. He's figured out how to send the right subconscious messages to his brain that enhance his creativity. He sees his songwriting as less of a writing process and more of a sculpting exercise, one that reveals what he hears within the music he writes. "I think every piece of music has something apparent in it lyrically. For me it's like fate knocking on the door. . . . It's like Michelangelo sculpting marble. Inside that marble is the sculpture, he's just got to find it. That's how I write lyrics. I write music and then ask, 'What does this music say to me?'"[14]

Here is one of our generation's greatest pop music songwriters saying, "This is how I work." He is not saying, "Here is how you should do it, too."

What is *your* process? What is the optimal setup for you to produce your best work? It's worth figuring that out, so that you can put yourself in a position to perform at an excellent level consistently. A valuable element of self-awareness is truly developing a sense of your own personal creative process—what works for you. Billy Joel discovered his. You have one, too. It's your job to find it. And when you do, integrity demands that you stay true to it. Trust yourself and your own personal excellence process.

CHANGE YOUR MIND

Being true to yourself and your own personal ideas, beliefs, and processes doesn't mean you should be resistant to ever changing them. Such intellectual inflexibility is the telltale sign of confirmation bias: the tendency to interpret new evidence as confirmation of your existing beliefs or theories. People who suffer from confirmation bias support or oppose a particular issue and will not only seek information to support their position but will also interpret news stories in a way that reinforces their existing beliefs. Over time, people become less likely to engage with information that challenges their views, and when they do, confirmation bias causes them to reject it.

According to Robert Sapolsky, professor of neuroscience at Stanford University, we tend to perform the process of gathering evidence and forming opinions in reverse. "We first come to a desired conclusion—often based on things as fleeting as group affiliation or life experiences. Only then do we look for evidence, and only the kind that supports our ready-made position."[15] It is because this trait is such a fundamental aspect of human nature that its opposite—the ability to change one's mind when the stakes are highest—is a real differentiator.

In 1983, Guy Kawasaki was hired by Apple to serve in a role that the tech world now would call Chief Evangelist. After four years of working in the world Steve Jobs had created, Kawasaki ventured out on his own to start several of his own companies. By 1995, he was back at Apple as an Apple fellow, working closely with Jobs, as he had before.

"One of the most important lessons that I learned from Steve Jobs is that changing your mind, changing what you're doing, reversing yourself at an extreme," Kawasaki told *CNBC Make It* at the Synergy Global Forum, "is a sign of intelligence. It's a sign of competence."[16]

Kawasaki explained what this looked like in practice. When the iPhone debuted in 2007, its software environment was a closed system. To protect the integrity of Apple's front-to-back, software-to-hardware design ethos and the system's security, Jobs refused to allow outside developers to create apps for use on this new revolutionary fusion of the cell phone, the mp3 player, and an internet-connected computer. If software developers wanted to build apps for use on the iPhone, they would have to build those apps using a Safari plugin.

After only a year, that decision was proving to be a disaster. For all the potential of the new iPhone, its capability was being choked off by this restrictive barrier to innovative app development. In response, Jobs made a complete "180-degree reversal," Kawasaki says, opening the iOS environment up to outside developers.

The lesson is one that remains with Kawasaki to this day, and one he imparts to others from his perch as the chief evangelist at the free-to-use online graphic design site, Canva. "When you figure out you're doing something wrong, don't try to bluff your way, don't try to perpetuate a mistake. You'll actually do yourself a favor, probably the organization you work for, probably your boss, too, by changing your mind, by reversing—by fixing what's broken."[17]

Brad Feld has been an early stage investor and entrepreneur since 1987. Growing up, his parents gave him positive affirmation for being curious. When I asked him to share the advice he gives to the startup founders he works with, his answer focused on biases. "People often defend their biases instead of questioning their biases." He's learned to approach new ideas with a Buddhist philosophy: by letting go of assumptions and approaching each topic with a beginner's mind. This mindset has helped him raise north of $500 million for his venture capital business, Foundry Group.[18]

When I think about the most impactful leaders in my life, they are the ones who had the confidence and humility to realize when they were wrong and change their mind. Only the strongest and clearest thinkers can do this. As Julia Galef, author of *The Scout Mindset*, told me, "You should take the approach that you're wrong. Your goal is to be less wrong."

The ability to think and rethink what you know to be true is a superpower. The ability to change your mind will make you a better decision maker. The ability to ask, "What is a better way to do this?" will help you perform more optimally in the long term. We've all heard, "We've always done it this way" from a boss before. Don't be that person. Be the one who says, "Wow, I've never thought of it that way. Thank you for opening my eyes to something new." It doesn't mean the new way will be right. It just means you will be open to it being right.

CHOOSE TRANSFORMATIONAL RELATIONSHIPS

The people you intentionally choose to have in your life will play a bigger role in your long-term excellence than perhaps any other choices you make.

One of the guests I've had on the podcast whose work I find myself coming back to again and again is Brent Beshore. Brent is the CEO of Permanent Equity, a firm that specializes in investing in "boring" (their word)[19] family-owned business. Recently, Brent shared a snippet from a private investor letter that perfectly captures an important idea about the purpose of our relationships:

> Transactional people often have a single goal in mind in their relationships—to benefit themselves and look out for their own interests, often at the expense of others. Everyone they encounter serves as a means to an end, whether it is an introduction, to sell you something, or to raise money. Visualize high pressure salespeople, politicians, media-seeking CEOs, or someone you barely know who reaches out for a quick ask. When you are no longer

useful to them, they drop you, because there is only loyalty to you in the moment. Their definition of success is based on the here and now, not the long road ahead. If you enter the relationship assuming a long-term outlook, you will find later that you have paid a kind of tax rather than invested in a friendship.

Transactional CEOs may appear wildly successful, but the ones who got there using shortcuts will soon face real problems, likely followed by stagnation or fast decline. Their attitude is do whatever it takes and deal with consequences later. Because their success was built on a weak foundation, they end up with lawsuits against them, enemies, scandals, and other problems, having never built a sustainable business. Therefore, if you are a long-term investor, you must avoid investing in transactional leaders. You simply cannot compound transactional relationships.[20]

There is a significant difference between mutually beneficial long-term relationships and a series of transactional relationships. We know transactional people exist, but we can be fooled, especially if we lead with trust. Be on the lookout for people who exhibit these qualities when you encounter them:

- **Constant name droppers.** They use big names as a way of building credibility.
- **Scant attention to details.** They focus more on "getting a win" than in seeing that win all the way through to complete implementation.
- **Always selling.** Though I am a proponent of the sales profession, we must remember that sales is about solving problems, not pushing a product or service to someone who may not need it.
- **Lots of talk, little action.** Transactional people make a lot of promises, but often do not deliver on them.
- **They do not invest in relationships.** They show up only when a person is useful to them.

- ▶ **False flattery.** They often resort to generalities; the key to a genuine compliment is specificity (e.g., "I loved the opening story you told in the town hall meeting. It applied perfectly to our situation.").
- ▶ **Self-promotion.** They overuse "I" and rarely say "we."
- ▶ **Lack of integrity.** If someone is willing to break the rules to win or to help you, they'll be willing to do it to hurt you at some point.

I'm not advocating that you become a cynical person who constantly questions the sincerity of others. But it's worth your time to be aware of transactional people and minimize those relationships in your life. Surround yourself with people who genuinely want to see you do well and for whom you want the same. You increase your odds of living a life of excellence.

To better understand the difference between a transactional relationship and a transformational one, I reached out to a number of my most trusted friends and asked them the makeup of the great relationships in their life. Here are a few of the qualities of a transformational relationship:

- ▶ **Transformation.** By definition, you are transformed by these people. They change you. They make you better. They are willing to push you beyond your current boundaries, and because of that, you get better. You do the same for them.
- ▶ **Trust.** As CEO of Insight Global, Bert Bean told me about his friend and Chief Revenue Officer, Sam Kaufman, "My trust in Sam is *marrow deep.*"
- ▶ **Humor.** This came up more than I expected in responses from friends. Your transformational friends have the right to make fun of you, and you spend a lot of time laughing together. This stems from trust and love.
- ▶ **Vulnerability.** There is no facade, there are no walls. They have the confidence in themselves and trust in you to be 100 percent

real. They share secrets, insecurities, and problems. And you do the same.

- ▶ **Respect.** There is a mutual respect for the value that each person brings to the relationship. Transformational relationships are built on complementary qualities that each person respects and appreciates in the other. When I was working on my MBA, my friend Jameson Hartke played the role of a tutor for me. He had a degree in finance and understood most (or all) of my coursework better than I did. I respected his knowledge of a complex subject and willingness to teach me. He was new to the profession of sales at the time, and I was in a leadership role. I tried to help him become a better sales professional. We had complementary skills that benefitted each other.

- ▶ **Gratitude.** They compliment people behind their backs. When you're talking with these types of people, they are constantly shining a light on the goodness of others. When something goes well in their life, they are quick to point out how it couldn't have been done without the great work of other people.

- ▶ **Optimism.** Regardless of the circumstances, they believe that they'll figure it out and things will go well. And they feel the same way about you. They are willing to take the extra step to help you fight through any challenges you are facing.

BUILD THROUGH DIALOGUE

Having one-on-one conversations is a critical tool in building transformational rather than transactional relationships. The care, curiosity, honesty, integrity, and compassion you show will determine whether or not you build long-term meaningful relationships. Transformational relationships are those that change your life. The care, presence, and wisdom of the other person makes you feel better and more fulfilled. I've thought about this a lot in the context of conducting my podcast interviews. I sincerely want to build relationships with my guests beyond the formal interviewer-interviewee dynamic. Here's what I've learned after conducting more than 500 interviews.

Prepare

For a podcast interview, I read everything my guests have written, watch videos of all their speeches on YouTube, and review articles others have written about them. Using this information, I build a full 360-degree view of them and write my interview outline accordingly. One new part of preparation that I've added to my repertoire over the past year is reaching out to mutual friends and asking them one simple question, "What is something I should know about them that I can't find on the internet?" This has elicited all types of interesting responses.

As I was preparing to interview rocket scientist Ozan Varol, I reached out to our mutual friend, Shane Snow. Shane said, "Ask him why he still rents DVDs on Netflix instead of just streaming them." That seemed bizarre. So I asked Ozan about it. He laughed, and then gave a thoughtful answer about the benefit of delayed gratification and the careful planning process he has with his wife of choosing a movie (to watch together) and then having to wait a few days to do it. Their feelings of anticipation are important to him. He enjoys the buildup and likes strengthening his ability to wait.[21] This one question asked by a mutual friend made our conversation much better. Those little tidbits of information and dialogue are critical elements to building meaningful relationships with the people on my show. I want them to remember me for being thoughtful, curious, and unique. I want them to want to continue the conversation beyond the one interaction on my podcast.

Now, obviously, the preparation for a podcast interview is different from what you would do for normal, real-life interactions. For someone you're meeting for the first time and haven't had time to prepare for, the plan is simple: be intentional with the questions you ask. Most interactions start with small talk. If there is genuine curiosity, the conversation can go in unexpected and fun directions. In some cases, you may want to skip the small talk (does the weather really matter?) and ask questions that will elicit more interesting answers. Something like "What excites you most about your work?" or "What's your secret ambition?" I also love the "champagne question," which I learned about at an event hosted by Jayson Gaignard. "If we were to meet up 365 days from now with a bottle of champagne, what are we celebrating?" Instead of having a lot of conversations at the surface level, choose to have fewer conversations, but each one having more depth.

Start in the Back

When speaking with someone who has written a book, I turn first to the acknowledgments before digging into the substance of the book. I search for names of people that mean a lot to the author and consider starting with a question about one of them. Since I do my interviews on Zoom, I can see their reaction to my questions and can get a sense of their emotions right away. I have not always done it this way. In earlier interviews, I typically started with: "What are the commonalities among leaders who sustain excellence?" While I still like that question and ask it frequently, I don't typically open with it anymore. I did it in the past because I wanted to start the conversation with substance. Now, I like to open with a question about love, specifically a person they love. The goal is to get them out of interview robot mode and into a more emotional place. I want them to feel different and more open. When I interviewed Admiral William McRaven, I opened with a question about his parents and followed up with one about the influence of a high school football coach whom he had written about and how impactful that person had been. I was talking with a military war hero (he headed the mission to capture/kill Osama bin Laden, as well as the rescue of Captain Phillips, among many other missions), but I wanted him to start from a place of love and openness so we could have a deeper conversation.

How does this apply outside the world of interviewing people? You can do the same in any interaction with another person. Ask about important people in their life, the ones they love. Ask about what they've learned from them, the impact they've had, what they've taken from them that they now teach others. This quickly changes the conversation from a surface-level rote exercise to a much deeper experience. The payoff of this approach is more meaningful relationships. The path to an excellent life is made possible by people and their willingness to share their hard-earned wisdom with you. Then you, in turn, can share it with others. We are all the sum of our experiences. I want to learn about those experiences from others. To be interesting, you must be interested in others.

Listen

People want to feel seen and heard. To ensure that, listen to them. Really listen. All the way until the end. Not the I'm-just-waiting-until-you-finish-so-I-can-talk type of listening. I mean giving them your full attention until they've stopped speaking. Only then, after they have finished their thought, do you start formulating your next question. The most impactful questions are follow-ups. Those questions are built from something specific said by your counterpart. Specificity matters. Listen with intent and respond to what they've said.

When you make people feel heard, you will increase your odds of deepening your relationship with them more quickly than usual. I have long advocated for what consultants Jack Zenger and Joseph Folkman call "listening like a trampoline." Here is how they describe it: "While many of us have thought of being a good listener, being like a sponge that accurately absorbs what the other person is saying, instead, what these findings show is that good listeners are like trampolines. They are someone you can bounce ideas off of—and rather than absorbing your ideas and energy, they amplify, energize, and clarify your thinking. They make you feel better not merely passively absorbing, but by actively supporting. This lets you gain energy and height, just like someone jumping on a trampoline."[22]

I try to play the role of a vessel for the ideas and useful techniques that I have learned from many others over the years. These one-on-one connections have had as big an impact on my life as any other actions I've worked to implement.

I believe that finding purpose and meaning leads to mental and physical health and a life well lived. Embracing a growth mindset allows you to strive, thrive, and improve. Being willing to question yourself and fix what is broken keeps you from getting stagnant, defensive, and closed off. And building transformational relationships increases your odds of good company on your pursuit of excellence.

2

FOCUS AND DISCIPLINE

*The common denominator of success—the secret of every
person who has ever been successful—lies in the fact that they
formed the habit of doing things that failures don't like to do.*
—ALBERT E. N. GRAY

Eliud Kipchoge holds the official world record for the marathon at
2:01:39. Of the 13 officially sanctioned marathons that Kipchoge has
run, he's won 11. He is the only known person to ever run the 26.2 miles
of a marathon in under two hours (in an unsanctioned event).[1] In the running community, Kipchoge is called "The GOAT" (greatest of all time).

Born in Kenya, he was raised by a single mother and only knew
his father from pictures. He did not start training seriously until he
graduated from secondary school in 1999. So how did a man go from
such a humble start to being the best in the world? To find out, I spoke
with Alex Hutchinson, a runner, scientist, and the bestselling author
of *Endure: Mind, Body, and the Curiously Elastic Limits of Human
Performance.* We spoke at length about Kipchoge and his model of
excellence.[2] Here are four of the big takeaways I took from our look at
the greatness of Kipchoge, captured in the words of the runner himself:

1. **Discipline = Freedom.** "Only the disciplined ones in life are
   free. If you are undisciplined, you are a slave to your moods and
   your passions." I know it feels counterintuitive, but for Kipchoge,

discipline is his path to freedom. Some people have the tendency to self-sabotage and let external influences (the media, politics, or other factors outside of their control) impact their work. Staying disciplined and sticking to the plan and the daily process of improvement creates real freedom. Kipchoge's daily work frees him from the limitations that would bind him, absent that work. The same can be true for you.

2. **Mindset.** "Athletics is not so much about the legs. It's about the heart and mind."[3] Kipchoge believes that training your mind is equally important to training your body. He told the BBC that "the mind is what drives a human being."[4] Throughout his training, Kipchoge internalizes his goals and cements them as something he truly believes he's capable of achieving. That belief creates confidence and becomes a self-fulfilling prophecy. He is proof that people can will themselves to improve and perform at high levels.

3. **It's about the team.** "You cannot train alone and expect to run a fast time. There is a formula: 100% of me is worth nothing compared to one per cent of the whole team. And that's teamwork. That's what I value."[5] From the outside, most people view running as an individual sport. Not Kipchoge. His training sessions are always with a team. He surrounds himself with other disciplined runners, trainers, and coaches to help him improve. He understands the value of being surrounded by others who lift him up. It is notable that he celebrates the excellence of his friends. When one of his training partners, Geoffrey Kamworor, won the New York City Marathon, Kipchoge was there at the finish line to congratulate him. Kamworor would later share that he was motivated by Kipchoge's presence at the finish line. "I knew my training partner and mentor Eliud was waiting at the finish. I was concentrating because I did not want to disappoint him."

4. **The results take care of themselves.** "To win is not important. To be successful is not even important. How to plan and prepare

is crucial. When you plan very well and prepare very well, then success can come on the way. Then winning can come on your way."[6] Kipchoge's sole focus is on his process to improve. The results take care of themselves. A look at his marathon times reveals that even as he approaches the age to be considered a "Masters athlete," Kipchoge is getting faster. He's improving. He's not focused on others. He's focused on continually improving himself. He cares more about his own personal best times than other runners' records. He's always striving to break his own personal records, not those of others.

Kipchoge is a prime example of someone who came from a modest background and worked to become the best in the world at what he does. While it may be easier for some than for others, it is possible for all of us. The potential for excellence is within all of us. The ones who achieve it and sustain it are intentional about their daily, disciplined process to make it happen. Those who, like Kipchoge, focus on the heart, the mind, and the continuous process to improve can create real freedom.

3.9 AND 4 FLAT

Mike Trout has been one of baseball's best players from almost the moment he broke into Major League Baseball (MLB) as a 19-year-old. Over the course of his nine full seasons, Trout has been an All-Star eight times, the American League's Most Valuable Player three times, and MVP runner-up four times. In fact, Trout finished either first or second in the MVP race in each of his first five years in the majors and has never finished lower than fifth.[7] In other words, every single season Trout has played he has been among the top of his sport. He is an all-time, transcendent talent.

But none of these accomplishments are what he wants to be known by. In a recent interview with baseball writer Peter Gammons, Trout talked at length about the oddest of statistics: the time it takes to run to first base. A scout with the Toronto Blue Jays had scouted Hall of Fame Milwaukee Brewer Robin Yount in 90 games over a five-year period. During that time, the fastest the scout ever timed Yount running from home to first base was 3.9 seconds; the slowest was 4.0 seconds. Trout loved that. He loved it when his idol Derek Jeter once asked Gammons to never again praise him (Jeter) for running hard to first because "what's so hard about running hard four times a day?"[8]

Trout had his coach with the Los Angeles Angels go through all of his recorded home-to-first times. It took the coach a few days to gather the data. When he did, the results were identical to the legendary Yount: consistently between 3.9 seconds and 4.0 seconds. "I don't care about the other numbers, WAR (wins against replacement), OPS (on base percentage plus slugging percentage)," said Trout. "When you think about me, I hope you'll think about 3.9 and 4 flat."

What's interesting to me is that Mike Trout can point to many impressive statistics that he's racked up over his career, and yet he doesn't. He's known as one of the greatest baseball players of all time, and yet he is focused on how to play the game the right way. This applies to so many areas of life. When someone looks at my work, I want them to say, "He gave everything he had to positively impact the lives of others. He did it the right way." This is something my wife, Miranda, and I try to teach our children. Do the right thing. Do it the right way. Leave people, places, and things better than you found them. You see trash on the ground, pick it up. A friend needs help, help them. Your team needs you, be there. Your child asks you to go to the park at 8 a.m. on a Wednesday, go to the park. Will this person, this place, or this thing be better because of me? Let the answer always be yes.

WHAT IS YOUR WALL?

Heading into the London Olympics in 2012, Michael Phelps was at the height of his powers as the most dominant swimmer in history.

Four years before at the Olympics in Beijing, Phelps won gold in all eight events in which he competed. In doing so, he broke Mark Spitz's record from 1972 for the most gold medals won in a single Olympics, as well as setting the record for the most career gold medals by any single Olympian, with 14. His performance in Beijing was not only perfect from the perspective of the medal stand; it was record-breaking. Of his eight gold medal swims, seven set new world records and the eighth (100-meter butterfly) set a new Olympic record.[9] Arriving in London in 2012, Michael Phelps was the personification of unbeatable.

Until he wasn't.

In the final for Phelps's signature event, the men's 200-meter butterfly, South African Chad le Clos shocked himself, Phelps, and the rest of the world by out-touching Phelps at the wall for the gold. The margin of le Clos's victory was razor-thin: five hundredths of a second. It had been over a decade since Phelps had lost in the 200-meter butterfly event at the World Championships or Olympic level.[10] During an interview with Bob Costas after his last event at the London Olympics, Phelps announced he was retiring from competitive swimming. "This was the last medal I will ever swim for," he said, holding up one of his four gold medals.[11]

Phelps's retirement didn't last long. By 2014, he was back, but with no mention of the next Olympics. Even more to the point, Phelps was clear: he would never compete in the 200-meter butterfly event again.[12] A year later, he finally acknowledged that he had his sights set on returning for his fifth Olympic games: the 2016 games in Rio de Janeiro, Brazil. His loss to le Clos in London and "his (lack of serious) preparation for those London Games" fueled his desire to return. In a media report that May, Phelps announced he had changed his mind about the 200-meter butterfly as well. He would be back to race that after all, noting the relatively static nature of the times that were winning the 200-meter butterfly when compared to those in 2000 when Phelps made his first Olympic appearance. "It's still not that fast an event," he said.

Phelps's remarks captured the attention of le Clos, who was not shy about his eagerness to beat the great Michael Phelps again. While at the World Championships, le Clos responded with bravado: "He's been talking a lot of smack in the media about how slow the butterfly is, so I just can't wait until I race him." In another interview, le Clos ramped it up even more: "Next year [at Rio] is going to be Muhammed Ali–Joe Frazier. Look, I don't want to say it's easy to swim by yourself [against lesser competition at the US Championships than at Worlds], but it's a lot harder when you know Chad le Clos is coming back at you the last 50 meters. That's what he's got to think about really."[13]

The buildup for the Phelps–le Clos rematch in Rio was tremendous. In the warm-up room before their semifinal event, the broadcast captured Phelps staring intensely from under his hood and headphones at le Clos, who appeared loose and at ease while shadowboxing in front of where Phelps sat. The image quickly went viral as an instant classic meme: the Phelps Death Stare. The finals race the following night did not disappoint. The two competitors were in adjacent lanes: Phelps in lane five, le Clos in lane six. At the halfway point, Phelps held a half-second lead over le Clos, who was in third place. By the third and final flip turn, le Clos was in second, but the gap between him and Phelps had grown to two-thirds of a second. At the finish, Phelps had reclaimed his Olympic title, barely holding off the second-place swimmer from Japan by four hundredths of a second. Chad le Clos, the defending Olympic gold medalist, finished off the medal podium, in fourth place.

As the swimmers came down the stretch for the last 25 meters, photographer David Ramos captured an iconic photo. In it, you see le Clos looking to his left, watching Phelps as he is pulling away. And Phelps? He's staring directly at his target: the wall. The time for Phelps to be focused on le Clos had been the day before in the warm-up room. At the moment of truth, there in the pool, Phelps's gaze had a singular focus: on getting to the wall first and winning the gold medal.

Le Clos, like many of us in our daily lives, divided his focus. Instead of focusing singularly on his stroke and using it to get to the wall as fast as possible, he gave away moments of focus to check on his rival swimming next to him. The result? He went from second place to no medal.

Having a singular focus is a fight each day. In a world of never-ending alerts and the ability to get whatever we want from an app

(A ride? Uber. A meal? DoorDash. A date? Tinder. A vacation rental? Airbnb.), we are in a constant battle against distraction. But excellence requires discipline in where you put your focus. A divided focus, sometimes even for just a split second, is enough to make you miss your mark.

HOLD ON TO THE FISHING POLE

John Chambers served as the CEO of Cisco Systems from 1995 to 2015 and as the company's executive chairman from 2015 to 2017. During his tenure, Cisco's annual revenues ballooned from $70 million to $40 billion. Suffice it to say, he's had one of the greatest CEO runs in the history of business. When I had the opportunity to talk with him, my goal was to figure out how he did that. When I asked him, he started the answer in a place I never would have expected: West Virginia in the summer of 1955.

John shared an old memory: he was just six years old and standing on the banks of the Elk River, fishing with his father. Even though John was a good swimmer for his age, his dad still cautioned, "Now, as we fish, I want you to stay up on the bank. Don't get near the edge. Because if you get swept in, it could be really dangerous." After about a half hour of fishing, instead of taking his dad's advice, John let his curiosity get the best of him. He went too close to the water and fell into the river. "I slipped off the rock. I was in the water, and I started to panic. I was getting just plummeted across the rocks and getting bruised, and the current was really fast. For a second, I thought, 'I might die.' And all of a sudden, I looked up and my dad was coming down the side of the river as fast as he could run on the rocks."

As the current pulled John downstream, his dad yelled, "Just hold onto the fishing pole!" This seemed like a strange command at the time; the fishing pole was a cheap old thing—"it was an ugly fishing pole and couldn't have cost five dollars." But John figured, "Obviously, if he was worried about me losing the reel, I was in no danger. So I grabbed ahold of that reel and rod with both hands, and every time I surfaced, I got a breath of air. I could see him running down the bank, trying to catch up, and I'd go back underwater."

Finally, John and his fishing pole ended up in a shallow, slow-moving section of the river that enabled his dad to catch up to him and pull him from the water. That's when John's dad "set me down on the bank, made sure I was alright, and then he walked me through what he had just taught me. He said, 'Do you know why I told you to hold onto the fishing pole?'" Of course, six-year-old John had no idea. John recalled: "He said, 'When you get into real trouble . . . you've got to be very careful not to let panic set in. And you can't just say be calm. You have to be able to focus on what you can control and influence. You've got to deal with the situation. You've got to size up how serious it is. And then you've got to be able to work your way into calmer waters.'"

"That was pretty dangerous," his dad summarized, "and your mom is going to kill me when I tell her what happened. But this is how you do it."

"I think I got it," John said, assuring his dad.

"Are you comfortable?" John's dad asked him.

"Yes, I am," John answered. And at that, his dad put him back into the river and "down the rapids I went again!" John told me. This time, however, John could follow his dad's advice with understanding and intention as his dad walked along the bank. "I did exactly what he said. I got calm. I put my feet out in front of me in the rapids because that way you could hit off the rocks with your feet. And when [I got] pummeled, I didn't panic; [I] just came back up and got more air. And then I waited for a slow spot where I could swim out. I had that lesson in life forever. It was one of the best teaching moments about dealing with stress, dealing with crisis management, and being realistic that there will be a tendency in all of us—no matter how brave you think you are—to panic. And that's what gets you into trouble."[14]

It's a great metaphor for life and applies to us all. When we strive for excellence, there will inevitably be bumps and dips along the way. Sometimes the adversity takes a form that is more than just inconvenient; sometimes it feels like an existential crisis where survival itself is at stake. We must be able to hold onto the fishing pole, to focus on what we can control as we strive to see the world as it is and work to find our way to calmer waters. When adversity strikes, as it inevitably will, we have a choice. How will we respond? Remain calm within the chaos? Or lose focus and panic? Your choice will likely determine the result. What will you choose to focus on?

SHOW UP CONSISTENTLY

The natural question is, "OK, but how do I do that? What can I do to improve my focus?" After years of interviewing some of the world's most effective leaders for my podcast, *The Learning Leader Show*, and analyzing their habits and behaviors, one concept seems to stick out more than most. These high achievers focus on the daily action rather than the results. They commit to the process.

People regularly ask me, "How can I build a big podcast following and create a business off of that following?" My answer always starts with this: I love each part of the process of my podcast. I love the act of preparing for a long-form conversation. I love the process of developing better questions, becoming a better listener, and asking even better follow-up questions. I love searching for and finding fascinating guests with whom to have conversations. I get a thrill from reaching out cold to highly influential people and having them respond that they'd like to come on my show. The entire process is rewarding and fulfilling work. None of these involve a focus on the end goal of having a podcast with a tribe of fans large enough to support a career. Instead, they are all just the daily acts of the work. Devote yourself to the process of doing those things well, and the good outcome will come find you.

Occasionally, people will ask me to help them launch a podcast, and I routinely respond by asking them a simple question: "Why?" Often, the answer is along the lines of "I think it's a good marketing tool to help me get more keynote speaking gigs or acquire more clients." At that moment, I know that the podcast won't last. It's too hard. It's too time consuming. I've seen too many launches begin with great excitement only to become menial labor. Soon after, it's the end of the podcast.

High achievers who hit what they are aiming at do so because they fall in love with the process, not an outcome. If you don't love the process and the daily actions required to excel, your odds of achieving what you've set out to accomplish are very low. Before setting a goal, think about the daily actions it will take to achieve that goal. Are those actions something you can fall in love with? If not, rethink your goal, for down that road lies not excellence but drudgery.

Talkers Versus Doers

One of the easiest ways to keep yourself focused on the process and not on the outcome is to not be a "talker." My parents had a rule: My brothers and I grew up playing sports, but they never talked about our sports accomplishments with others. If people complimented my parents on the athletic feats of their children, they would say "thank you" and then shift the conversation to something else. Talking about the outcome wasn't important.

We've all met people who will tell you what they're "about to do" who then never quite get around to seeing the job through to its completion. And then there are those who just go do it and let others talk about what they've done. If you do great work, then it will speak for itself. Let your work do the talking for you. If your work adds value to the lives of others, people will share it. Let them talk about the outcomes you are producing while you remain focused on the process that produces them.

When I started my podcast, I committed myself to this approach. I told only a few people of my intentions before I started: my wife, my brother, and my good friend Greg Meredith. Then I set out on the process of building: cold-emailing potential guests, setting up the digital infrastructure, diving deep into researching those guests who'd agreed to my ask, and recording my conversations with them. I had 22 episodes recorded before I published the first one. Until then, nobody except those few within my close circle knew what I was up to.

Derek Sivers is a man who has accomplished many goals. He was the founder and CEO of CD Baby, an online distributor of independent music, which he eventually sold for $22 million. He then took those proceeds and donated them to an organization he created to fund music education called The Independent Musicians Charitable Trust. In 2010, he gave not one TED talk but three.[15] Derek knows a thing or two about setting goals and achieving them, so I paid particular attention when he told me, "You should keep your goals to yourself. Tests done since 1933 show that people who talk about their intentions are less likely to make them happen. Announcing your plans to others satisfies your self-identity just enough that you're less motivated to do the hard work needed."[16] In his TED talk on this topic,[17] he stresses the context: "These studies are only about identity goals: goals usually related to personal development, that would make you a slightly different person if completed. This does not apply to things like starting a company, or other pursuits where it would be useful to corral a bunch of people to support your project."[18]

When it comes to the ambitious project of improving yourself and pursuing excellence, keep your focus on what matters: the work to be done. Be the type of person who just does the work, not the one who wastes time and energy telling people what you're about to do. As Benjamin Franklin said, "Well done is better than well said."

LEARN THE SMALL STUFF TO DO THE BIG STUFF

Jeff Estill is a friend and former colleague who served the United States as an Army Airborne Ranger–qualified infantry officer and deployed to Iraq with the 82nd Airborne Division in the years after 9/11. We often talk about leadership and compare notes and experiences we've accumulated on our very different paths. During one of these conversations,

I described the fundamentals of quarterback play and why focusing on basic footwork and hand movements is critical for setting the foundation for success as a passer. Jeff responded by sharing with me why it's vital that a person never loses sight of the fundamentals of how to do the job of the people they are leading. "A general might never need to use an M-16, but there is a clear expectation that they know how to shoot it, maintain it, and understand its capabilities as well as any private."

"What do these fundamentals have to do with excellence?" I asked.

"One of my best experiences as a paratrooper," Jeff answered, "was with a battalion commander, Lieutenant Colonel Larry Swift, who had brought in a completely new way to clear a room. He learned it from doing it. And he had the power and command to say, 'This is how we are going to do it across our battalion.' And then we got down to doing the work." Respect for Jeff's commander flowed from his fundamental knowledge of a standard operating procedure. Because this commander had spent time actually doing the work, he knew how to create a better way, and his soldiers did more than just obey: they *bought in*.

Over the last few years, I have been fortunate to interview members of the Special Forces community, from individual operators to generals with command authority. In the military, senior leaders are simply expected to know and understand the basic tasks of the work of the battlefield. Without this knowledge, it is challenging to lead with excellence. They are expected to know what needs to be done and understand how to prioritize. Without a fundamental knowledge of each task, this is hard to do.

Jeff is now a senior executive at a Fortune 50 company. When I asked him how he takes what he learned as a Ranger to his work in corporate America, he said, "Unfortunately, a lot of people just go day to day and pick something up by osmosis and their knowledge set gradually expands. But the most effective people are aggressively learning their trade and have extra motivation to move themselves forward."

In the business world, it is rare to find in a person with positional power the fundamental knowledge of the actual work done by direct reports. Leaders with this knowledge are incredibly valuable to an organization.

As Jeff has experienced, this is recognized and respected. When I asked him for the most common feedback he receives from his peers, he told me, "Oftentimes, I'm the least tenured person in the meeting, so for those who don't know me, the expectations may be low, but they invariably say, 'I can't believe how much you know about this.'" For Jeff, it's just part of his process for improving what he learned in the military. "In the military, there are a lot of regulations. The people who really know what they're doing actually read the full documents of the regulations. I mean the actual manuals, the actual equipment. In my job, there are a lot of written policies that are written by lawyers. And I read all of them. I print them out, highlight them, and scan them back into my One Note file. It's hard. It takes a long time, but it gets me there. Most people aren't willing to do that. Most just show up to work. I take pride in knowing what I'm supposed to do. I hate not knowing what's going on. So I do the work to ensure that I do know what's going on."

Pursuing excellence is having the willingness to do the necessary work to develop a deep understanding of a topic from a foundational level. Having the desire to be a value-enhancer to the people around you is what excellence is about. I want others to say, "I want him on my team. He makes our team better. He makes everyone around him better." Isn't that what we all want? If so, we need to be willing to do the foundation-level work to ensure we "know what's going on."

NO CHEAP TRICKS

Chase Jarvis is a world-renowned, award-winning photographer who has worked with some of the world's most recognized brands such as Apple and some of the world's most recognizable people such as Serena Williams. He is also the founder and CEO of CreativeLive, an online learning platform on which top experts teach creative skills. When a fan asked Chase for the "tricks" someone could utilize to do what he's done, he gave what was likely a very disappointing answer. "It's ruthless discipline. There are no tricks. The focus part is what's wildly misunderstood. When you are focused on doing a thing and you do that thing relentlessly until you get the outcome you want, it's celebrated. No one else sees the other stuff. My best work has always come through discipline and focus."[19]

I learned more about the absence of tricks from Brook Cupps, who described his mantra of "Chop Chop" (think: chopping wood). He explained, "I never viewed myself as talented or really good at anything, I've just always been able to find my way because I've worked. I'm willing to do what needs to be done. I learned that from my parents growing up. We were low-middle class. You just had to work. My dad would get up every day, whether he was sick or healthy. It didn't matter. If it was a weekday, he got up and went to work. Chop Chop is that connection back to work. When things are good, you work. When things are bad, you work. Trusting that that process will eventually pay off. The loyalty and discipline to buckle down and do what you need to do."

MOKI MARTIN: THE LESSON OF THE SUGAR COOKIE

The discipline of focus works best when it is aimed at what is within your control. Simple to say, harder to execute. Keeping your focus on what you can control like, say, your reactions to circumstances rather than the circumstances themselves, becomes exceedingly difficult precisely when it is needed most.

During my podcast conversation with Admiral William McRaven, he shared with me the story of a friend of his named Moki Martin. The two men first met when McRaven began his training to become a Navy SEAL.

> When you go through SEAL training, the instructors are king. Whatever they say, you gotta do. No matter what it is. If they don't like you, they can just tell you to "hit it!" You have to run

fully clothed over the sand dunes, jump in the Pacific Ocean. You come back and roll around in the sand. You throw sand down your shorts and your shirt. You are completely covered in sand. The effect is called a sugar cookie.

Well, one of the instructors that used to harass me unmercifully was a Navy lieutenant named Moki Martin. Moki was a former enlisted who had become what we call a limited duty officer. Just a remarkable SEAL: a highly decorated Vietnam vet, very professional, very capable. He could do everything well. Every time Moki would see me in SEAL training, he'd point me out and say, "Mr. Mac, hit it!" And I think, oh man!

Once Lieutenant Martin asked me if I knew why I was a sugar cookie, and I said, "No!" And Lieutenant Martin said, "Because life isn't fair." So interestingly enough, when SEAL training was over, he and I ended up on the same team. And we became very good friends.

In the early 80s, Moki was out riding his bike. He was a hell of an athlete, and he was prepping for a triathlon. He's riding his bike from Coronado down to Imperial Beach, and he has a head-on bicycle accident. He ran head-on into another guy on a bicycle. And the other guy gets up, kind of dusts himself off [and walks away]. And Moki was paralyzed from the chest down and has been for the last 37 years. And never once in those 37 years have I ever heard Moki Martin say, "Why me?" Never once has he said, "Gee, life's not fair." Because the lesson of the sugar cookie going through SEAL training was just that. It was a recognition that life's not fair. There were some guys who went through training and thought that if they finished first on the run, somebody oughta pat them on the back and tell them how great they were, and when that didn't happen, they didn't understand. But that was the lesson. "Hey! Life's not fair. Get over it." And Moki Martin to this day, he never whined once, he never said, "Why me?" He went on to be an accomplished painter, he fathered a child, and today, he supervises the UDT SEAL triathlon that they do every year in

Coronado. I saw him about six months ago, and he's as effervescent and as charismatic and as fired up as ever. It's a wonderful story.[20]

In your career, you will see others get promoted whom you feel don't deserve it because they are not as accomplished as you. This happens in every industry. Spending your personal energy thinking, "That's not fair" is a waste of time. If you live long enough, you'll see bad things happen to good people and good things happen to bad people. It's one of those inevitabilities of life. Spending time and energy worrying about what's out of your control is destructive.

Once Moki Martin was paralyzed, he had a choice. He had to face the question that faces anyone who has had to deal with the cosmic unfairness of tragedy and injustice: Do I want to make something of my life? Or do I want to complain and ask, "Why me?" It would have been perfectly understandable if Moki had chosen the latter. But he didn't. Instead, he decided to focus on what he could control and making the most of his life.

This is one of the important life lessons my wife and I try to impart to our children. We tell them, "You can control two parts of your day today: your attitude and your effort. Focus on showing up with a great attitude. Bring positive energy to the rooms you enter. Be a value-add for the others you're with. And give maximum effort. You can control how hard you try. You can control the attitude you have while doing it. If you're going to do it, then you might as well give it 100 percent. If not, then don't do it. Better yet, do it with a smile. Bring positive energy to the room. If you focus on those two things, your attitude and your effort, you'll find yourself in a better position day after day."

CONSISTENCY: KEEP HAMMERING

Steve Martin dropped out of college to pursue his dream of working as a comedian. His first job in the business was as a writer for *The Smothers*

Brothers Comedy Hour. In the 1970s, he performed stand-up comedy in local clubs and wrote for *The Sonny and Cher Show.* In his book *Born Standing Up,* he writes about the critical insight he gleaned from those hard days early in his career that ultimately catapulted him to superstardom. "I learned a lesson: It was easy to be great. Every entertainer has a night when everything is clicking. These nights are accidental and statistical: like lucky cards in poker, you can count on them occurring over time. What was hard was to be good, consistently good, night after night, no matter what the abominable circumstances."[21]

I take an immense amount of pride in publishing a podcast episode every Sunday night at 7:00, no matter what. I've done that for six years. It's important to me to publish my "Mindful Monday" email every Monday morning at 9:00, with no exceptions. No matter what. It's about having integrity with myself. I do what I tell myself I will do. I understand that my work has become part of the routine of my listeners and readers. I must show up for them. And that is one of the reasons my work has caught on with so many people. They trust me. They know I'm reliable and consistent and I will show up, no matter what.

The San Antonio Spurs have been one of the model franchises in professional sports, winning five NBA championships over the last two decades. One of the main reasons why has been their leadership consistency: Gregg Popovich has been their head coach since 1996. He is the longest tenured active head coach of a single team of any of the major American sports leagues. In the Spurs' locker room hangs a quote by the nineteenth-century journalist Jacob Riis: "When nothing seems to help, I go and look at a stonecutter hammering away at his rock, perhaps a hundred times without as much as a crack showing in it. Yet at the hundred and first blow it will split in two, and I know it was not that last blow that did it, but all that had gone before." When pursuing championship goals like the Spurs do, it is critical to keep focused on the task at hand. Each day's effort doesn't get the job done in and of itself. But they stack up over time. It is through the consistency of the hammering that the championship stones are cut.

IF YOU'RE NOT EMBARRASSED,
YOU WAITED TOO LONG . . .

One of the most paralyzing thoughts when attempting to do something of excellence is the fact that your first effort will likely be bad. First day playing guitar? Probably horrible. First day working as a sales rep? You'll probably mimic the worst clichés of the used car salesperson everybody hates. First day on the football field? Not pretty. First writing draft? Embarrassing. The only way to improve is to do the work, knowing you will be terrible at it and doing it anyway. And then continue to do it again. And again. And again.

Kevin Kelly cofounded *Wired* magazine in 1993. He's also a bestselling author and has the justified reputation as one of the clearest thinkers around when it comes to the future of technology. For Kelly, sustained excellence comes from people who "cultivate, create, make, and have an ability to see the world a little differently."[22] For his sixty-eighth birthday, he wrote an article titled "68 Bits of Unsolicited Advice" that went viral. One of Kelly's bits of advice caught my attention: "To make something good, just do it. To make something great, just redo it, redo it, redo it. The secret to making fine things is in remaking them."[23]

He is right. Mark it down: you will come to a point where you will think, "This is pointless. I'm going to stop. It's too hard. My work isn't any good." Everybody feels this way, and that's when most people quit. But the demands of excellence require something harder: choosing to continue despite the struggle, amid the doubts, and in defiance of the imposter syndrome raging in your head.

John McPhee is one of the pioneers of creative nonfiction writing. He's a four-time finalist for the Pulitzer Prize, winning it once. In his book *Draft No. 4: On the Writing Process*, McPhee shares the importance of consistently keeping at it. "The way to do a piece of writing is three or four times over, never once. For me, the hardest part comes first, getting something—anything—out in front of me. Sometimes in a nervous frenzy I just fling words as if I were flinging mud at a wall. Blurt out, heave out, babble out something—anything—as a first draft.

With that, you have achieved a sort of nucleus. Then, as you work it over and alter it, you begin to shape sentences that score higher with the ear and eye. Edit it again—top to bottom. The chances are that about now you'll be seeing something that you are sort of eager for others to see. And all that takes time."[24]

By plowing forward and trudging ahead through the work that you know isn't very good at the moment, you create signals of progress for your mind. That progress then becomes the fuel to keep going further. The progress is inspiring and drives the internal motivation to continue. As I write this book, I set daily goals for progress. I set a goal to write 100 words a day. Even though 100 is not enough to hit my word count goal for the entire book, it feels like progress and it's doable. While there are days when I barely scratch out 100 words, there are others when I cruise past 1,000. It's about creating a habit and a manageable goal that drives me to continue to show up day after day. I think, "I know I can get to 100. Let's get going." And then I sit down and work. Once I start, I have a much better shot at hitting that long-term big goal than if I hadn't started. Get started, redo it, and keep going.

3

RESISTANCE

*It is not in the still calm of life, or the repose of a pacific
station, that great characters are formed. The habits
of a vigorous mind are formed in contending with
difficulties. Great necessities call out great virtues.*
—ABIGAIL ADAMS TO HER SON JOHN QUINCY ADAMS,
IN THE MIDST OF THE AMERICAN REVOLUTION

From the beginning of recorded history through May 6, 1954, the fastest any human being had ever run a mile was 4:01.4—four minutes, one second, and four-tenths of a second. There was no reason any person needed to run a mile faster than that. Nothing important in life hinged on running 5,280 feet fast enough to turn that leading four into a three. But the same can be said for pursuing excellence: the standard of "good enough" becomes a barrier that resists being broken. To chase excellence means to confront that resistance and push beyond it. So it was with the four-minute mile. Runners from across the globe had been focused on breaking that barrier for nearly 70 years, all to no avail.[1] And then came Roger Bannister.

The most remarkable aspect of Bannister's barrier-breaking run of 3:59.4 was how unexpected it was for that runner on that day to be the one. As Bill Taylor, cofounder of *Fast Company*, writes, the "experts" had long believed breaking the four-minute barrier would require ideal running conditions: "It would have to be in perfect weather—68 degrees and no wind. On a particular kind of track—hard, dry clay—and in front of a huge, boisterous crowd urging the runner on to his best ever performance." But on May 6, 1954, Roger Bannister had none of those things working in his favor. The day was cold, the Iffley Road Track in Oxford was wet, and the crowd was small at "just a few thousand people."

On top of that, Bannister himself was hardly the picture of a singularly focused athlete intent on breaking this imposing barrier. The bulk of his time was devoted to being a medical student. He was "an outlier and iconoclast—a full-time student who had little use for coaches." He didn't train like a maniac and sprint miles every day. He was notorious for doing the opposite: training for just one hour per day. Bannister did not go on to become the greatest middle-distance runner in the world. Instead, he finished his studies and became a neurologist.

How did this happen, and why does it matter?

First: Rather than employ an all-out training push that would have required him to sacrifice his studies, Bannister applied a scientific approach to training. He treated each race like an experiment. "Improvement in running depends on continuous self-discipline by the athlete himself, on acute observation of his reaction to races and training, and above all on judgment, which he must learn for himself," he wrote.[2]

Second: He believed the impossible was possible. Bannister was known to close his eyes and visualize the race, step by step. He would create the image, see the finish line, and hear the crowd—all in his mind. What separated Roger Bannister was that he believed he could do it. Runners had been attempting to break the four-minute mile since 1886. John Bryant, a British runner and journalist, wrote, "For years milers had been striving against the clock, but the elusive four minutes had always beaten them. It had become as much a psychological barrier as a physical one. And like an unconquerable mountain the closer it approached, the more daunting it seemed."[3] Bannister focused just as much time on conditioning his mind as on conditioning his body. "The mental approach is all important, because the strength and power of the mind are without limit," he wrote. "All this energy can be harnessed by the correct attitude of mind."[4]

The proof that the impediment to a sub-four-minute mile was psychological rather than physical lies not with what Bannister accomplished that soggy May morning in Oxford but with what happened after. Just 46 days after Bannister's historic feat, John Landy, an Australian runner, not only followed Bannister past the four-minute barrier, he bested it by over a full second: 3:57.9.[5] Before a calendar year had passed after Landy's record, three more runners broke the four-minute mark *in the same race*. The current world record time for the mile sits at 3:43.13, set in 1999.[6]

In their book, *The Power of Impossible Thinking*, Wharton School professors Yoram Wind and Colin Crook devote an entire chapter to Roger Bannister's feat in which they pose the following questions: "Was there a sudden growth spurt in human evolution? Was there a genetic engineering experiment that created a new race of super runners? No." The answer to what Bannister had achieved was not physical. "What changed was the mental model. The runners of the past had been held back by a mindset that said they could not surpass the four-minute mile. When the limit was broken, the others saw that they could do something they had previously thought impossible."[7]

There are four-minute-mile barriers in all our lives. Where are they in yours? What seems impossible but isn't? While you are misusing your energy believing it can't be done, the Roger Bannisters of the world are busy getting it done. Who would you rather be? All your energy can be harnessed by the correct attitude of the mind.

JANUARY 1 IS THE NEXT DAY

On December 31, 2020, I was flooded with the message: "FINALLY, this year is OVER!" But what changed? Nothing. I'm writing this amid the Covid-19 pandemic. Here in the United States, our world started changing in early March 2020. There was so much uncertainty, fear, and doubt. No one with any decision-making power had been alive the last time something like this had happened: the Spanish flu pandemic of 1918. The changing of the year did not change any of this. It did not change the death and destruction that continued on January 1. It did not change the damage that had already been done to small businesses that would continue into the following year. Were we getting closer to a vaccine being widely distributed? Yes. Were we closer to the end of the pandemic than we had been nine months ago? Of course, but not because the calendar flipped by one day. The change from 2020 to 2021 simply meant that another day had passed. An arbitrary day on the calendar did not mean that things were different.

And it certainly didn't mean *you* would be different. "All of my plans for the future involve me waking up tomorrow with a sudden sense of discipline and adherence to routine that I have never displayed even once in my life," writes author Rachel McCarthy James.[8] I'm with her: I don't understand New Year's resolutions. January 1 is a random date on the calendar. In order to make a change, you must make a choice: to implement the different habits and routines needed to accomplish the change you desire. A study by researchers at Scranton University found that only 19 percent of individuals keep their resolutions. Most of these decisions made with the best of intentions are abandoned by mid-January.[9]

What can be done about this? How can we get better at building the habits, rituals, and routines needed to overcome the resistance that stands between us and our pursuit of excellence? Over the past several years, I have had the great fortune of getting to sit down and discuss this challenge with James Clear, author of the number one *New York Times* bestselling book *Atomic Habits*. Of the many ideas I have learned from those conversations, here are three techniques for making change now and making it last:

Set Small Goals

As Leo Babauta puts it, "Make it so easy you can't say no." To complete the manuscript for this book, I had a tight timeline. From the date I agreed to the book deal with McGraw Hill to the time I needed to deliver the manuscript, I had just over three months. I will note that leading up to the deal, I had already begun writing the book, but it was far from complete. To get it done, I needed to write about 550 words per day. So I set a "words-written-per-day" goal for myself. What was it? 550, right? No. My goal was 100 words per day. "Ryan, how could that be your goal? If you hit it every day, you would miss your target date." Yes, that is correct. However, I understand my mentality when it comes to goal setting. I love to crush goals. I want to blow them out of the water. And I like to set realistic goals. Because getting up early and writing 100 words in a morning is not hard. Here's the thing. Once I write 100, I always keep going. The average number of words I've written per day since starting my daily writing habit to get this book done is over 600 words. Setting a goal of 100 words per day ensures that I'll turn on the computer and get the words out. Spending that time writing only 100 words is much better than writing no words. There are days when I don't write much more than 100. But there are other days when I go well over 1,000. My goal is set to ensure I do the activity that needs to be done in order to hit the long-term goal. The friction with most hard activities is at the beginning. It's starting. Once you start running, it's easier to keep going than it was to get started. You've created momentum that carries you. "Make it so easy you can't say no." It is hard to say no to a goal of just 100 words.

Aim for the Ritual

The issue with New Year's resolutions (and goals in general) is that people seek a result instead of a ritual. "Here's the problem," James Clear told me. "New goals don't deliver new results. New lifestyles do. And a lifestyle is not an outcome, it is a process. For this reason, all of your energy should go into building better rituals, not chasing better results. If you want a new habit, you have to fall in love with a new ritual."[10] A new ritual could be something as simple as a nightly journal practice or a dedicated morning routine.

Fix Your Environment

Dr. Benjamin Hardy is an organizational psychologist and bestselling author of *Willpower Doesn't Work* and *Personality Isn't Permanent*. When I spoke with him about changing our habits, he told me, "If you want to achieve your goals, you need to change your environment."[11] If you want to stop eating sugar, then get rid of all food with sugar from your house. You want to stop watching TV? Remove it from your room. Our actions are a response to the environment we put ourselves in. Most of us don't like to admit that we don't have willpower, but instead of trying to increase willpower, fix your environment. Surround yourself with the type of people you want to become. Show up in rooms with thoughtful people who are wiser than you. Remove the distractions and create an environment to increase your odds of behaving in a way that will help you achieve your longer-term objectives.

By doing these things instead of making resolutions, you give yourself great odds of finally achieving the change you have been chasing. Stanford professor Scott Sagan said, "Things that have never happened before happen all the time." All it takes is embracing the rituals of change and beginning the work on whatever date on the calendar today happens to be.

PROGRESS HAPPENS IN UNCERTAIN TIMES

As you stand at the precipice of the unknown, wondering if committing to the long-term path of change and embracing new daily rituals will get you there, Ozan Varol suggests asking yourself two questions: "What's the worst that can happen?" and "What's the best that can happen?" Varol explained to me, "Adopt an experimental mindset. Frame your actions as experiments. Don't be afraid to try new things."[12]

"Who is Ozan Varol?" you may ask. He is a law professor at Lewis & Clark Law School in Portland, Oregon, who, prior to pursuing a law degree, was a bona fide rocket scientist. A native of Istanbul, Turkey,

Ozan grew up in a family with no English speakers. He moved to the United States by himself at 17 years of age to attend Cornell University and major in planetary sciences. With his degree in astrophysics, Varol was a member of the operations team that launched the two Mars exploration rovers, *Spirit* and *Opportunity*, in 2003. He is the author of one of Amazon's Top 20 Business Books of 2020, *Think Like a Rocket Scientist: Simple Strategies You Can Use to Make Giant Leaps in Work and Life*. Varol knows a few things about taking a leap of life-altering change in the face of uncertainty.

Ozan and I recorded the episode for his appearance on my podcast during the pandemic. It was a fitting setting: "All progress happens in uncertain times," he told me. "It's bizarre. People prefer certainty of bad news instead of the fear of the unknown. Instead, be curious about tomorrow." When I asked him where his willingness to courageously leap into the unknown comes from, he said, "It takes courage . . . Oftentimes, there is a failure of courage. Have the courage to take action when the rest of the world is standing still." While I'm not certain that all progress happens in uncertain times, I believe that most progress happens at the edges of our zone of comfort and competency. And creating a habit of pushing those edges leads to growth as a result.

Uncertainty and adversity will inevitably be part of your life. How will you choose to respond—by aggressively investing in bettering yourself or by hunkering down and holding on tightly to the gains of the past? Like Ozan Varol, ask yourself two questions: What's the worst that can happen? What's the best that can happen?

THE PAIN OF THE PROCESS IS THE POINT

"Writing is a neuron-pumping activity that challenges your brain to translate shapeless ideas into logical, syntax-conforming sentences," writes Kaleigh Moore, an in-demand freelance writer and coach. "It's mental gymnastics when you have to take a fuzzy concept and transform it into words. . . . it forces you to work on sentence structure, composition, and general idea communication . . . It helps you understand yourself better, as you get to see your ideas translate from a vague concept inside your head to words and phrases on a page. It forces you to externalize your inner monologue. . . . As you write down your ideas, you'll fine-tune how to logically present ideas as you sort through translating your thoughts into words. [Through writing], you'll challenge yourself to make sense of things, rather than leaving ideas as gray, ambiguous concepts inside your head."[13]

Pursuing excellence requires clear thinking about good ideas, and writing is a critical component. Think of it as the exercise regimen of clear thinking. Creativity expert Todd Henry once told me, "I like having written. I don't like the process of writing." Who does? It is not only hard work, it is humbling. Most of us don't appreciate how little we know about something until we have to write what we know down. The picture is made clearer through the grueling process of capturing what's swirling inside our head and wrestling it down onto the page.

On my board in my office is a quote to remind me that writing a book is a painful process. I need this reminder because it is easy to confuse the pain of the process with that other kind of pain, the one that tells us something is very wrong. There's an illustrative quote from philosopher Alain de Botton: "Of many books, one feels it could have been truly good, if the author's appetite for suffering had been greater."[14] Suffering. Embrace it and continue despite it. The process of writing is one of those painful journeys by which logic is applied to thought that leads to clarity. It's worth the pain. Just as with the physical effort of exercise, the mental effort of writing is where the growth occurs. It is through this discomfort that one battles with what famed author Steven Pressfield calls "the Resistance." Pressfield claims the Resistance doesn't have a personal vendetta against anyone. Rather, it is simply trying to accomplish its only mission. It is the force that will stop an individual's creative activity through any means necessary.

Of course, this isn't just about writing. The process of straightening out our thoughts and ideas through the mental combat of writing is just a relevant and useful example. The notion that the pain of the process is the whole point is true for many of the challenges we face in life. Developing a vaccine? Painful process to get there. Earning a promotion to CEO? Painful process to get there. Dealing with a medical ailment? Pain and suffering is a constant. Those who understand it and keep going are the ones who perform at excellent levels far more consistently than those who quit. There is a reason why all math teachers require us to show our work—it's proof that we understand the process enough to replicate it in the future. Embrace the process, show your work, and demonstrate to yourself and others the competence you've gained.

THE HANDSTAND COACH

A big piece of overcoming the resistance that stands in the way of your pursuit of excellence is having a realistic view of your goals and what is required to hit them. Amazon founder and CEO Jeff Bezos once told a story about a friend who wanted to learn how to do a "perfect handstand." Initially, Jeff's friend took a workshop and practiced, but was not making progress. "So, she hired a handstand coach. Yes, I know what you're thinking, but evidently this is an actual thing that exists," Bezos wrote in his 2017 annual shareholder letter.[15]

The handstand coach gave Bezos's friend a bit of wisdom that applies to far more than just mastering the perfect handstand. "'Most people,' he said, 'think that if they work hard, they should be able to master a handstand in about two weeks. The reality is that it takes about six months of daily practice. If you think you should be able to do it in two weeks, you're just going to end up quitting.'" Unrealistic expectations can be as fatal to great achievement as having no expectations at all. This lesson resonated with Bezos.

Most of us can picture that boss who set outrageously unrealistic goals for us at the beginning of the year, served up with a "Shoot for the moon; even if we miss, we'll end up in the stars" attitude. But the whole point of the handstand coach's wisdom for Bezos is that this approach is foolish. If a leader is not honest with the team about what it takes to achieve a goal, that can diminish the likelihood of achieving it. "Unrealistic beliefs on scope—often hidden and undiscussed—kill high standards. To achieve high standards yourself or as part of a team, you need to form and proactively communicate realistic beliefs about how hard something is going to be—something this coach understood well," Bezos wrote. This matters because having high standards is a learned skill. "People are pretty good at learning high standards simply through exposure," says Bezos. "High standards are contagious. Bring a new person onto a high standards team, and they'll quickly adapt."[16] Conversely, blindly equating unrealistic expectations as "high standards" will kill that ethos just as quickly.

As a sales manager at LexisNexis, I was given an overall goal that my sales team needed to hit to finish the year at 100 percent of plan. While I didn't always agree with the goal I was given, I was grateful that I enjoyed the autonomy to choose how to allocate the responsibility for hitting that overall number among the 16 people on my team. When I started, the age-old advice shared by some of the long-term managers was, "Oh, I see you have four superstars. Just load them up with a lot of that number. They'll hit whatever you set for them."

This advice particularly struck a nerve with me because it was a philosophy I had formerly resented when I was one of the top-performing sales reps. While I was fortunate to usually be placed in a "target-rich" sales territory, the goal I was given didn't always correspond to what was realistically achievable. I made a note to myself that when I became a manager, I would not do this. I would not saddle my superstars with a disproportionate part of the team's total goal. My reason was simple: I did not want to penalize high performers for their skill, work ethic, and historical performance. That's not how you build a successful and sustainable business. Instead, I worked hard to create sales territories that were reasonably balanced with opportunity, setting similar goals for every person on the team.

Prior to giving my team their goals for the year, I would talk one-on-one with each person to explain my philosophy on goal setting. It would go something like this: "I am very grateful to have you on this team. You have shown that you are a high achiever. That said, your goal is going to be very similar to all the others on the team. Why? Because I'm not going to penalize you for your past excellent performances. In fact, I want to reward you for it, and incentivize you to continue to overperform. Also, I know you're not going to slow down once you exceed your monthly goal. You're a person who gives it your all through the end of each month, with the constant mindset of surpassing your goal. This is good for you and good for our company. My hope is that you'll be inspired by this reasonable goal, strive to achieve it, and ultimately exceed it month after month in the coming year."

This strategy helped propel my team to perform at levels higher than our region had ever achieved before and was a motivating force for top performers throughout the business. My team became a self-recruiting machine. Whenever I had an open position, team members would actively recruit their high performing friends from other companies to join them. High performers tend to hang around other high performers. Those are the people I wanted recruiting for my team. This created a flywheel of overperformance for the team, the benefits of which were enjoyed by them and me in the form of compensation, awards, and promotions.

But the key point that may be mind-bending for some: Do not "over-goal" high performers and "under-goal" low performers. That is the path to lower standards all around by incentivizing low to marginal performance and penalizing the high achiever. I want the high achievers to be the happiest, most optimistic people in our organization. I want them to keep coming back year after year, performing at a high level and being richly rewarded. Similarly, low performers will either improve over time to become one of those happy achievers or they will self-select out. They will, as Jeff Bezos put it, either "adapt" to the high standards "through exposure" or those high standards will be the force that ejects them from the organization. But the path to get there requires having a firm grasp on what is realistic and achievable.

SURVIVING THE HANOI HILTON

This is not just the stuff of business performance targets. In fact, the more critical your mission goal, the longer the timeline required, the more arduous the road, and the more demanding the effort required for its completion, the greater the need for a properly balanced sense of optimism and realism. Perhaps the greatest exemplar of this truth comes from the loneliest of isolation cells in Southeast Asia and the inspiring example of James Stockdale.

At the beginning of America's involvement in the war in Vietnam, US Navy Commander James Stockdale oversaw one of the Navy's most storied fighter squadrons, the VF-51 "Screaming Eagles." It was CDR Stockdale who, after launching his F-8 Crusader off the deck of the *USS Ticonderoga*, dropped the first American bombs on North Vietnamese soil on August 5, 1964, after the Gulf of Tonkin incident. Just over a year later, on his third tour of duty, Stockdale was in command of Carrier Air Group 16 aboard the aircraft carrier *USS Oriskany*. On September 9, 1965, Stockdale's A-4 Skyhawk was shot out from under him after a successful bombing run. At that point he had flown nearly 200 combat missions. This would be his last. He was captured immediately after ejecting from his plane, having suffered a broken bone in his back and a badly dislocated knee.[17]

For the next 90 months, Stockdale suffered the horrific tortures and deprivations of the famed Hanoi Hilton POW camp. As the highest-ranking officer among the prisoners of war held there, Stockdale led their cooperative effort to resist their captors' plans of being used as propaganda pawns. Stockdale was physically tortured over 15 times (through a gruesome technique known as "the ropes"),[18] subjected to solitary confinement in a stark three-by-nine-foot cell for four years, and bound in heavy leg shackles for two years. Through it all, Stockdale managed to keep his fellow POWs motivated and focused on resisting. He devised a means of communicating through their confined spaces and enacted a code of conduct to which the fellow prisoners held each other accountable.

He even went so far as to take a razor to his own head and to bash his face with a stool to disfigure himself so badly that he could not be used by the North Vietnamese in a POW propaganda photo. His treatment finally improved after he nearly died by slicing his own wrists with broken glass shards to show his captors he would rather lose his life than cooperate. From that point on, the torture stopped. Nobody suffered "the ropes" again. After his release and return to the United States, Stockdale continued to serve in the Navy, retiring with the rank of Vice Admiral. He remains among the most highly decorated officers in the history of the United States Navy, with 26 personal combat decorations, and was the only three-star admiral to wear both the wings of a naval aviator and the nation's Medal of Honor.[19]

During his post-navy years, Stockdale spent time studying stoicism at the Hoover Institute at Stanford University, which is where his path crossed with famed leadership expert and business school professor Jim Collins. That encounter resulted in a conversation Collins famously recounted in his book *Good to Great*. In Collins's retelling, he just had to ask the war hero: How in the world did you not only survive your seven-and-a-half-year ordeal but do so without breaking in the process? "I never lost faith in the end of the story," Stockdale told Collins. "I never doubted not only that I would get out, but also that I would prevail in the end and turn the experience into the defining event of my life."[20]

After quietly trying to process such unbelievable steadfastness, Collins asked a follow-up question: What defined those who didn't make it? Stockdale didn't hesitate: "Oh, that's easy. The optimists . . . they were the ones who said, 'We're going to be out by Christmas.' And Christmas would come, and Christmas would go. Then they'd say, 'We're going to be out by Easter.' And Easter would come, and Easter would go. And then Thanksgiving, and then it would be Christmas again. And they died of a broken heart." Then Stockdale uttered the words that formed the basis for one of Collins's most recognizable contributions to the study of leadership and excellence, the Stockdale Paradox. Said Stockdale, "You must never confuse faith that you will prevail in the end—which you can never afford to lose—with the discipline to confront the most brutal facts of your current reality, whatever they might be."[21]

It is easy to see how negative thoughts and pessimistic attitudes can drag us down and keep us from overcoming the obstacles of resistance that stand between us and our goals, but it's even more important to recognize the dangers of unbridled optimism, untempered by the cold hard facts of reality. The most impressive part of surviving the Hanoi Hilton was that Stockdale didn't know where it would end. It was a grind each day without a fixed point.

When faced with a challenge, think about the example of James Stockdale and strike a balance between unshakable faith in yourself and a cold-blooded, clear-eyed view of the reality of your present situation.

KEEP TAKING ONE MORE STEP

How does someone overcome the challenge of 90 months of horrific treatment in captivity? You can't. An obstacle like that—7.5 years high—is too much to tackle all at once. It must be taken one day, one hour, one moment at a time. Once that moment has been overcome, it's on to the next one.

This is the message Alison Levine delivers, whether from the stage of a keynote address, from the pages of her bestselling book *On the Edge: Leadership Lessons from Mount Everest and Other Extreme Environments*, or via Skype during my conversation with her for the podcast. Alison is one of only 20 people in the world to have completed what is known as the Adventure Grand Slam. This achievement, years in the making, involves climbing the highest mountain peak on each of the seven continents and reaching both the North and South Poles *on foot*. She also served as the team captain for the first American Women's Everest Expedition. Even more amazing, Alison has spent almost 20 years doing all this, despite suffering from Raynaud's disease, a condition that "causes the arteries that feed her fingers and toes to collapse in cold weather."[22]

"What that mountain taught me is that everybody has that voice in their head that tells them they can keep going even when they feel like they can't," Alison told me. "When I was on that mountain feeling dehydrated, sick from the altitude, I thought, I'll just take one more step, one more step again, maybe one more? And then that voice kept saying one more, one more. I kept taking one more. And eventually I was at the summit. Everybody has that voice in their head. You just have to find it."[23] It's a message she reiterates to her audiences over and over. "You don't have to be the best, fastest, strongest climber to get to the top of a mountain," Alison writes. "You just have to be absolutely relentless about putting one foot in front of the other."[24]

"When one can see no future, all one can do is the next right thing," says Pabbie, the wise old Troll King in Disney's *Frozen 2*. This truth is about the need to focus on taking care of what is in front of us. While we need to look ahead as far as we are able, and mitigate risks where we can, we must recognize that the only reality is the moment we're in right now. Maybe you're out on a run and you feel like you can't go any farther. Set a shorter landmark and get there. When running a marathon, instead of thinking about all 26.2 miles, think about the next marker to hit. "The cups of water are 300 yards from here. I can make it there." Once you get there, set another landmark, and get there. Then do it again: continue setting short-term markers to hit, and then hit them.

The same is true for your business, your relationships, and your life. Focus on taking your spouse on an excellent date this Friday. And then the next one. And the next. String together the excellence. After a while, you'll look back and see the benefits of doing it consistently. Breaking down large goals into smaller pieces creates a better system for progress: think, "What can I do today to move toward it?"

MORTALS DON'T GET TO DETERMINE YOUR FATE

One last note about the resistance you will face in pursuit of excellence. There is plenty of it out there in the form of things you simply cannot ignore. No matter your mindset, the laws of physics will not bend to your plan; the economic laws of supply and demand will not yield to your business plan's best-case scenarios; and the flow of time will not allow you to go back and undo mistakes already made. Given this, follow the advice of Frances Frei and decide to "not let mere mortals define your life."

Frances is an award-winning professor at Harvard Business School and author of the book, *Unleashed: The Unapologetic Leader's Guide to Empowering Everyone Around You.* In 2017, Uber hired her to be the company's first ever Senior Vice President of Leadership and Strategy, with a mandate to help the company navigate the rough waters of its disastrous leadership and culture meltdown. Her TED talk from TED2018 on "How to Build (and Rebuild) Trust," recounting the challenge she faced at Uber, has been viewed nearly 5 million times.[25]

Among the many great topics of conversation I had with her, the one that stuck with me the most was about the road she had to travel to get to where she is now, the pinnacle of an excellent career. It turns out that the tenured HBS professor was originally rejected by Harvard, and not just once! She told me, "I've been rejected by Harvard five times in my life . . . as an undergrad, grad student, and as a professor multiple times. But I said to myself, 'I'm not going to let mere mortals determine my fate.' They are not going to define my life."[26]

Frances didn't hold a grudge. She didn't say, "Screw them, I'll go somewhere else." She wanted to be at Harvard and didn't take it personally when decision makers rejected her. She thought, "Well, I must not be telling my story in a compelling way." And she resolved to do the work, to get better, and not let other people's decisions seal her fate. She has since gone on to become a bestselling author and earn tenure at one of the finest institutions of higher learning in the world. If you want something bad enough, don't let "mere mortals" determine your fate.

PART II

THE FUEL

4

WHAT LIGHTS YOU UP

Nothing of me is original. I am the combined
effort of everyone I've ever known.
—Chuck Palahniuk

oward Thurman is a name you have probably never heard before. Born in Daytona Beach, Florida, in 1899, he grew up in a time when discrimination was legal and lynching was common. Howard's grandmother, Nancy, raised him after his father died of pneumonia when Howard was just seven years old. Nancy was of the generation of African Americans who had been slaves in antebellum America. She didn't know how to read or write. From these humble beginnings as an African American boy raised by an illiterate former slave in the depths of the Jim Crow South, Howard would later go on to graduate as Morehouse College's valedictorian in 1923. He became an ordained minister just two years later.

To many, Thurman remains unknown, yet he was one of the primary influences on one of the most influential leaders in American history. On Sunday afternoons, Dr. Martin Luther King Jr. would often stop by Howard's home to watch Jackie Robinson play baseball on TV. Howard was a classmate of Dr. King's father at Morehouse College, and he had a paternal relationship with Dr. King. Howard was the first African American pastor to travel to India and meet Gandhi. He shared what he'd learned from his time with Gandhi, ultimately inspiring

Dr. King to incorporate Gandhi's philosophy of nonviolent resistance into the civil rights movement. "One cannot understand King's philosophy and theology without first understanding Thurman's work and Thurman's influence on King and other civil rights leaders," says David B. Gowler, coeditor of *Howard Thurman: Sermons on the Parables*.[1]

One day, a young person whom Howard was mentoring asked him, "What does the world need me to do?" And before he'd finished his question, Howard interrupted: "Don't ask what the world needs, ask what makes you come alive, and go do it. Because what the world needs are people who come alive." It is a shift in thinking. Needs get filled and problems get solved. These are examples of what Simon Sinek describes as "finite games"—those pursuits that have a defined end point at which "winning" is possible.[2] But people giving their life to the work that makes them "come alive" is a resource without limits. It is playing an "infinite game" in which being "ahead" or "behind" replaces "winning" and "losing," and the competition is not another person, company, or market—it is only themselves in the past. The pursuit of excellence requires operating the same way.

LOVE VERSUS WILL

Legendary comedian Jerry Seinfeld described this well in a conversation with radio icon Howard Stern. Howard said, "I thought, you know, it is possible to will yourself, maybe not to be the greatest in the world, but certainly to get what you want." Jerry responded, "I'm going to adjust your perspective a little bit. That was not will. What you were using, what Michael Jordan uses, and what I use is not will. It's love. When you love something, it's a bottomless pool of energy. That's where the energy comes from. But you have to love it sincerely. Not because you're going to make money from it, be famous, or get whatever you want to get. When you do it because you love it, then you can find yourself moving up and getting really good at something you wanted to be really good at. Will is not like not eating dessert or something—that's just forcing yourself. You can't force yourself to be what you have made yourself into. You can love it. Love is endless. Will is finite."[3]

I love hosting a podcast. Outside of time with my family, having a long-form, one-on-one conversation with a thoughtful leader is my absolute favorite thing to do. It's number one on my list (even ahead of working out or swimming in Lake Tahoe, two activities I love very much). Because I enjoy it, I want to be great at it. I want to work at it. I want to study the craft of being a better interviewer. I love finding fascinating people and asking them to be on my show. All of that is part of the process. The more I work on my interview skills, my odds of becoming excellent at interviewing increase. And I am willing to do all that work—the work that necessarily happens behind the scenes and hidden from view—because I genuinely love the work.

This might be why it is common to hear people say, "Find what you love, and you'll never work a day in your life." While I understand the sentiment, it's not accurate. While I am blessed to do what I love for a living, it is most certainly work. The commitment to a daily habit of writing is work. The 10 to 15 hours of preparation before a podcast recording is work. Putting myself out there in the form of cold emails to potential guests is work. Developing a presentation for a keynote speech is work. Practicing that presentation for hours and hours by myself in my home office, hotel rooms, and in front of coaches is work. And, of course, there is the selling of my services (keynotes, one-on-one clients, leadership circles, The Learning Leader Academy). Without sales, the business dies. All of that is work.

The reason I do it all is because I love it. I love the process. I love the feeling of building momentum and experiencing growth. Of pushing the edges of my comfort and competency zones. Of producing quality work that impacts the lives of others. I love the email I received recently from a farmer in southern Illinois who told me that *The Learning Leader Show* is a topic of conversation at his dinner table each night.

Brian Koppelman asked world-class songwriter Shane McAnally, "Do you picture a son or a daughter taking in your song with their dad?

Does that help you write songs?"[4] This question made me think of how I picture my work being consumed. Who gifts my book to someone? Why? What do I hope they feel? What connections are being formed by my work? How does it bring people together? How does the sharing of my work build community? Will two completely different people love my work so much that it brings them together? That is powerful. That is inspiring. That fuels me to keep going, especially on a blazing Tuesday afternoon when I pull the shades down to block the hot sun and I'm trying to come up with the right words for the next sentence.

That is my fuel: the love of the craft. The love of the work is the driving force behind it. It is not the force of my will. Will isn't strong enough for all the work. It's love. Think about how you want others to experience your work. How is your team impacted by your actions today? How are your peers impacted by what you produce? By how you treat them? By the questions you ask? And so, I ask: What is your fuel? What do you love doing more than anything else? Don't ask what the world needs; ask what lights you up and go do that.

DIE EMPTY

In the year 2000, Todd Henry was in a work meeting with colleagues when a question was posed by a guest they were hosting that day. The guest asked, "What do you think is the most valuable land in the world?" Todd's was a typical response: "Ahhh, I don't know . . . oil fields in the Middle East? Gold mines in South Africa?"

The guest answered his own question with the words of the late Bahamian preacher Myles Munroe: "I believe the most valuable land in the world is the graveyard. Because in the graveyard are buried all of the unwritten novels, all of the untaken risks, all of the unlaunched business, all of the unexecuted ideas, all of the unreconciled relationships, basically all of the stuff we carry with us our entire lives that we never put into the world. We think, 'Well, tomorrow I'll get started, tomorrow's the day I'm going to take the first step,' so we push it into the future until one day we reach the bookend of our lives, and all of that value is buried in the ground, never to be seen by human eyes. That's why it's the most valuable land in the world. Because all of that unexecuted value was buried with us in the ground."

That day, Todd Henry went home and wrote two words on an index card and hung it up in his office. Those two words have defined the last two decades of his life: "Die empty." Todd told me, "Because I want to know when I reach the bookend of my life that I'm not taking my best work to the grave. That I'm doing everything I can each and every day to put that work into the world and be of value to others, and I'm building a body of work I can point to at the end of my life and say, Yes! That represents me. I want to make sure I'm not allowing myself to succumb to fear, apathy, or the paralysis that comes from uncertainty so that someday I can die empty of regret and full of satisfaction for a life well lived."[5]

Since that day 20 years ago, Todd has written five bestselling books, launched one of the first podcasts ever in 2005, and spoken on stages all over the world. Through his work, he has helped creative leaders do the best work of their lives. He inspires me to be intentional about my daily actions and strive to inspire others to be purposeful about living a life of excellence. Even if he stopped all his productive work today and didn't do anything except "eat, drink, and be merry" for the rest of his days, his life would still be judged as that of a productive achiever. But doing this would not be in line with the call to "die empty," so Todd presses on.

GET OUT OF THE SAND

Movement is life, and with it comes influence and impact on the world around you. Legendary leadership guru John Maxwell put it this way to me: "Good leaders adapt. They shift. They don't remain static because they know the world around them does not remain static." John's record speaks for itself. He has written more than 100 books that have been translated into 50 languages. In 2014, he was named the number one leadership expert in the world by *Inc.* magazine at age 67. Since earning that award at an age when most people are retired, he continues to write at least a book a year, selling millions of copies of each one. As if that wasn't enough work of influence, John does all this while also traveling the world, sharing his message with audiences in the tens of thousands. In 2020, he came on my podcast twice.

After all those accomplishments, and now at the age of 74, I asked him: "Why don't you relax on the beach and slow down a little bit?" He quickly responded, "Nobody wants to follow me when I'm sitting my butt in the sand."[6] John Maxwell is John Maxwell because he knows that excellence in leadership means constantly striving to improve yourself with the intent of helping others. Occasionally, I have a conversation with someone who says to me, "Jeff Bezos has all the money in the world; why doesn't he retire and relax?" The answer is that leaders like Jeff Bezos and John Maxwell are not wired to sit their butt in the sand. That's why they have what they have. Like sharks that must keep swimming to keep breathing, retiring to the beach or the golf course is not an option for those pursuing excellence. They are living to fulfill their potential, and that is endless. They have created wealth and fame because of that mindset. They wouldn't have acquired them without it, or without constantly raising the level of expectations. "No one ever coasted their way to greatness."

"Change is inevitable. Growth is optional. Today's ceiling becomes tomorrow's floor," John told me during our second conversation. "A difficult time can be more readily endured if we retain the conviction that our existence holds a purpose, a cause to pursue, a person to love, a goal to achieve."[7] Experience is not the best teacher. Evaluated learning from experience is the best teacher. The people who sustain excellence view change as an inevitable part of life. They don't hate it, they don't fear it; they understand it, and they keep going.

David Rubenstein is a great example of what John Maxwell was talking about. David is co-executive chairman of The Carlyle Group, one of the world's largest private investment firms. Since David cofounded it in 1987, Carlyle has grown into a firm managing $217 billion from 32 offices around the world. When I spoke to him, David was 71 years old. He told me, "I would give all of my money away to be just one year younger."

"Really?" I said, "You're a multibillionaire."

"Yes, of course! Everyone would. All we have is time. Time is everything. I would give everything for more time."

I paused for a second and thought about that.

David continued, "Many of my classmates from college and law school, they're retiring, and I am actually doing the opposite. Instead of slowing down, I'm speeding up."[8] He's doing everything in his power to maximize and make the best use of his time. Time is our most valuable resource. You can make money, but you cannot make time. The question is, how will you make the best use of it?

THE MOST USELESS QUESTION

"What do you want to be when you grow up?"

It's a question so common that we ask it and answer it without really thinking through it. In her book *Becoming*, former First Lady Michelle Obama writes, "I think it's one of the most useless questions an adult can ask a child—*What do you want to be when you grow up?* As if growing up is finite. As if at some point you become something and that's the end."[9] Her life is a case study in how false that view is. As she puts it, "So far, in my life, I've been a lawyer. I've been a vice president at a hospital and the director of a nonprofit that helps young people build meaningful careers. I've been a working-class black student at a fancy mostly white college. I've been the only woman, the only African American, in all sorts of rooms. I've been a bride, a stressed-out new mother, a daughter torn up by grief. And until recently, I was the First Lady of the United States of America."

The beauty of excellence is that it's the result of always striving to do better. It's not about comparing yourself to anyone but to your previous self. At some point, you might become a doctor or a lawyer or a teacher, but is that the end? Of course not. If you were familiar with my work at all before picking up this book, chances are you've heard me quote the words of NBA sharpshooter J.J. Redick, who captured this perspective so perfectly when he appeared on my show: "You've never arrived. You're always becoming."[10]

Instead of asking children what they want to be when they grow up, we should be focused on instilling the belief that there is no end to growth. There is no official "grown up" and finished stage in life. A few years ago, I flew out to Los Angeles to meet with the basketball coaching legend George Raveling. Here is the man who possesses the original copy of Dr. Martin Luther King Jr.'s "I Have a Dream" speech, helped Nike sign Michael Jordan, and was the first African American basketball coach in what is now the Pac-12.

As I walked into his office, a pair of young men who appeared to be in their late twenties met me at the entrance. "Coach Rav" (as he's known to friends) was 81 years old at the time of our meeting. I asked him whom he chooses to have in his life, given that he can essentially hang out with whomever he wants. He told me, "When you're 81 years old, you need four or five young mentors. They can help you navigate and understand the twenty-first century. You have to have the willingness to be vulnerable to the way they think. I have four or five of those people that could be my sons, but they are my teachers. I would say to all of those modern elders out there: if you really want to accelerate your growth, get four young dudes and let them be your mentors."

As I sat in Coach Rav's office, I was surrounded by stacks of books. Even at his advanced age, Coach Rav is still a voracious reader and learner. When I asked him why he reads so much, he said, "The slave owners used to hide money in books because they knew slaves would never look in the books because they couldn't read. If someone can control my mind, they can control my body. I will not let that happen." He continued, "My grandmother taught me to be curious. She taught me to ask. She taught me good manners. She taught me humility. She taught me to help people."[11]

The more I talked with him, the more Coach Rav reminded me of the Italian phrase *ancora imparo*, which means, "yet, I am learning." It is a phrase that is often attributed to the Renaissance master artist Michelangelo, who is said to have invoked the phrase at the age of 87 as a statement of his commitment to lifelong learning and artistic evolution. It's a lifelong commitment that animates how Coach Rav lives as well. "Information equals knowledge," he told me. "Knowledge equals wisdom. Wisdom equals opportunity. Opportunity equals growth. Growth equals success."

About a year and a half after that meeting with George Raveling, I was at the NCAA Final Four waiting backstage. I was about to go on stage to interview John Calipari (men's basketball head coach for the University of Kentucky) and Michael Lombardi (former New England Patriots executive and three-time Super Bowl winner). As we waited, the empty small talk started to turn toward the awkwardness that comes before the conversation completely stalls out into silence. Knowing that George Raveling is a beloved figure in the basketball community, I said to Coach Calipari, "Hey, do you know Coach Rav?"

At the mere mention of Coach Rav's name, the dynamic of the room immediately shifted. "Oh my gosh! I *love* Coach Rav!" Calipari gushed. "Have you met him?" I told him I had and shared the story about my recent trip to LA for my lengthy interview with Raveling. And even though Michael Lombardi's professional career was in football and not basketball, it turned out that he and Raveling were great friends. Lombardi chimed in with similar love for Coach Rav. In no time at all, the two men were engaged in a tennis match–like conversation, volleying Coach Rav stories back and forth. As I listened, the common theme of their stories was Coach Raveling's aggressive curiosity, his love of learning, and how he was always striving to do better. He's inspired so many by never believing that he's "grown up." Instead, even in his eighties, George Raveling continues to embrace the process of growing, and his excellence is simply the result of his always striving to do better. The impact that Raveling has had on these two excellent coaches was evident, as they continued to share Coach Rav tales right up until the moment we were announced and went on stage.

FIND YOUR EDISON

In 1896, Henry Ford was a 33-year-old engineer working in the newly developing electricity industry with the Detroit Edison company. That year, at the annual meeting of the Association of Edison Illuminating Companies, Ford was one of 44 men from the 18 power companies that were all associated with America's greatest inventor, Thomas Edison. With Edison seated at the head of the table, the conversation turned to the prospect of using electricity to power vehicles.

"There's a young fellow who has made a gas car," said one of the executives from Detroit Edison, pointing Ford out to Mr. Edison. The crowd at the table eagerly wanted to hear about the young man's project, which he had just completed and dubbed his "Quadricycle." Because Edison was nearly deaf at this time in his life (he was 49 years old), Ford had to move down and take a seat next to him. As Ford described his vehicle, Edison "brought his fist down on the table with a bang and said, 'Young man, that's the thing; you have it. Keep at it.'"

Three years later, Ford left the Edison family of companies and struck out on his own, making his gasoline-powered carriages a full-time pursuit. Less than a decade after that decision, the Ford Model T debuted and took America by storm, forever changing how journeys were undertaken and how machines were made. Ford would later describe that moment of encouragement from Mr. Edison: "[His] bang on the table was worth worlds to me. No man up to then had given me any encouragement."[12] The two builders became lifelong friends, even buying vacation homes near each other in Fort Myers, Florida. Their relationship would go on to span some 35 years, until Edison's death in 1931.

Economics professor and bestselling author Tyler Cowen told me, "At critical moments in time, you can raise the aspirations of other people significantly, especially when they are relatively young, simply by suggesting they do something better or more ambitious[ly] than what they might have in mind. It costs you relatively little to do this, but the benefit to them, and to the broader world, may be enormous. This is, in fact, one of the most valuable things you can do with your time and with your life."[13] For Cowen, it was suggesting to a couple of students who were applying for admission to his university's master's degree program that they apply for the PhD program instead. "At least two of our very best students went down this route. Neither realized that it was common simply to apply straight to a PhD program, skipping over the master's."[14]

Take a moment and think about the people who have played this role in your life. Who believed in you before you believed in yourself? Who lifted you to levels higher than you thought you could reach? Call them. Tell them. Go see them. Share a meal and reminisce. And make sure to say, "Thank you." Whenever I get the chance to do this, it always leaves me with a rush of positive emotion, and it usually does for my mentor as well.

I recently went out to dinner with my high school football coach, Ron Ullery. I've written a lot about the impact that Coach Ullery has had on me. His work ethic, attention to detail, and overall preparedness for every aspect of coaching a team inspired me to try to be more like him. His willingness to push me beyond what I thought I was capable of was driven by his love and care for my teammates and me. It meant everything.

Our wives joined us for a night out. At dinner, I looked him in the eye and told him the impact he had on me. I thanked him. And I told his wife, Lara, that her husband had changed my life. Coach Ullery gave that knowing nod of approval and gratitude. Even in this moment, at a dinner table so many years later, I still wanted to make him proud. It's amazing the impact mentors and coaches can have on your life.

Be that person for others. As Tyler Cowen said, it may cost you relatively little, but it could mean the world to others. Be intentional about whom you can help. And encourage them to aim a bit higher. To go for a little more. You never know the impact you could have on a person. What if you make a habit of doing this daily? Think about all the seeds you could be planting, and how cool it would be to see them bloom someday. Never doubt for a second whether it's worth it. It is.

There are many stories about athletes or entertainers using the doubts of "haters" as fuel to prove their detractors wrong. There will always be those who doubt you or make you angry or unhappy. As an alternative, why not wrap your arms around your supporters and work like crazy to prove them right? I think you'll find it's a more enjoyable way to live your life. Seek out your Edison and use that support as fuel to prove them right, as opposed to trying to prove the doubters or haters wrong.

Think of the people who believe in you—those who think you will succeed, who support you and give you encouragement and feedback. I am lucky to have people like that in my life. I hope you are, too. Prove them right. Turn your supporters into bona fide truth-tellers.

TURN YOUR FLYWHEEL

Herminia Ibarra is a professor of organizational behavior at the London Business School, where she studies how people make career transitions. Author David Epstein interviewed Ibarra for his book, *Range: Why Generalists Triumph in a Specialized World*, in which he examines why generalists may be better positioned for the coming future than specialists. "We learn who we are in practice, not in theory," Ibarra told Epstein. "We discover the possibilities by doing, by trying new activities, building new networks, finding new role models." Relying only on introspection doesn't work because our insight into ourselves is constrained by our roster of previous experiences. You actually have to act and then think—try things and then reflect on how they fit you and what they reveal about your abilities and interests. We learn who we are, as Ibarra put it, "by testing reality," not merely by looking inside.[15]

The mental model I employ for managing my own personal growth operates from this same principle. Learning is the fuel for that growth, but like any fuel, there is a process for getting the most out of it. Mine looks like this:

1. **Collecting.** By reading, listening to podcasts, speaking with mentors, watching keynote speeches, I take in new material

each day to fuel my curiosity to know more and to question my assumptions.

2. **Refining.** I do the experimentation that Ibarra and Epstein discussed. I take what I've learned, and I put it into action. I must always be in the mode of implementing what I'm learning. If I learn a new theory on how to run a meeting better, then I'm going to test that theory the next opportunity I get. I must have the mind of an experimenter and always be willing to try something new.

3. **Processing.** At this stage, I review the actions I've taken and the experiments I've done based on what I've learned. I analyze what worked, dig into what didn't, and work to understand why. What needs to change? What could I do better? Why did the experiment work or not? What will I continue doing that's new, and what will I stop doing? Reflecting on the actions I've taken is a critical step in the always-learning framework.

4. **Distributing.** One of the greatest tools for learning is sharing what you've learned with others. Nothing clarifies your understanding of a topic like trying to teach it to someone else. Sharing forces clarity through the process of preparation.

This framework of collecting new ideas, refining them through practice, processing what that reveals, and then distributing this to others keeps me constantly focused on both the theory and the practice of an idea. I can read forever on how to give an effective presentation. However, I will never actually be able to experience it until I stand up in front of a group of people and start performing. Putting my mind into the position of constantly experimenting helps me learn quickly and adapt to the ever-changing environments we are in.

What is your process to get clarity? What is your process to take action? How are you working with intention to take the raw materials of information and inspiration and turn them into the high-octane rocket fuel of personal growth that impacts others along the way?

5

THE POWER OF OTHERS

Humility is not falsely denying praise or discounting
your own self-worth. That's called lying. Humility is
understanding that you're but one person with one
perspective and that the world is a vast place.

—GAGAN BIYANI

In 1939, Bill Hewlett and David Packard launched their partnership as a formal company from Packard's garage in Palo Alto, California. Thanks to the flip of a coin, the friends decided that Bill's name would come first on the company letterhead, and the Hewlett-Packard Company was born, becoming Silicon Valley's "first major start-up company, and one of its most successful."[1] The partners' first product sale was to The Walt Disney Company, which bought eight of Hewlett-Packard's audio oscillators for use in the production of its animated film *Fantasia*. The total sale price for the eight devices was $572.[2]

Over the ensuing decades, as the company's impact and fortunes grew, Bill Hewlett kept the same modest office with the same dated furniture that reflected his preference for modest living. He was known for his penchant for "walking around" the various offices and labs where work was being done, a practice later immortalized by Tom Peters as "MBWA": Managing by Wandering Around. Hewlett led by being accessible and connected to people in his employ, in large part because that was how he was outside of work. Even 30 years after launching HP,

Hewlett's phone number remained listed in the local phone book for anyone to find. One day in 1967, a boy living in Palo Alto placed a call to the Hewlett home. The president of Hewlett-Packard answered the call himself.

"Hi, I'm Steve Jobs. I'm 12 years old. I'm a student in high school, and I want to build a frequency counter. And I was wondering if you had any spare parts I could have." As Steve Jobs would later recount, Bill Hewlett "laughed and he gave me the spare parts to build the frequency counter. And he gave me a job that summer at Hewlett-Packard, working on the assembly line putting nuts and bolts together on frequency counters. He got me a job in the place that built them, and I was in heaven."[3]

For the man who would go on from that summer job to help found Apple Computer, Inc., and become the icon for Silicon Valley success and the fusion of technology and design, this experience left a profound mark. "Most people don't get those experiences because they never ask. I've never found anybody who didn't want to help me if I asked them for help," Jobs would tell the Santa Clara Historical Association in 1994. "I've never found anyone who said no or hung up the phone when I called. I just asked. And when people ask me, I try to be as responsive and pay that debt of gratitude back. Most people never pick up the phone and call, most people never ask. And that's what separates the people, sometimes, who do things from the people who just dream about them. You gotta act. You gotta be willing to fail. You gotta be willing to crash and burn. With people on the phone, with starting a company, with whatever. If you're afraid of failing, you won't get very far."[4]

This lesson about simply asking for help is such a vital piece of pursuing excellence and personal growth that I want to spend a chapter exploring it. Just as Steve Jobs did as a young boy, I have had great experiences that came from being willing to reach out to people who don't know me at all and ask for their help. When I was a freshman at Miami University, I wrote an email to Drew Brees. At the time, I had no way of knowing that Brees would go on to not only play in the NFL but have a Hall of Fame career and a Super Bowl trophy on his award-filled résumé. I admired him and was impressed by how he led his team as a senior All-American quarterback at Purdue. So, much like Steve Jobs looking up Bill Hewlett's phone number in the phone book, I tracked down Brees's email address and asked him for advice on how to be a great quarterback. See Figure 5.1 for his response.

```
Subject:  Fwd: Re: fellow college qb, note from drew brees


>Original-recipient: rfc822;hawkrc@muohio.edu
>
>Well, Ryan, I wish you the best of luck at Miami.  Y'all should have a
>really good team during your time there, and have a chance to do
>something really great.  I guess my only advice to you is to set your
>goals high, but make them achievable.  This includes personal goals and
>team goals.  Because if you achieve your personal goals, in that
>offense, as it is in this offense, you will most likely achieve your
>team goals at the sae time.  Remember, the team revolves around you as
>the quarterback.  You can control the tempo and attitude that your team
>plays with.  This includes being very confident and staying composed in
>all situations.  It is OK to show emotion, but make sure it is positive
>and motivational.  Also, no matter what, always stay humble, because you
>are one of the lucky, but realize that you are also one of the best.
>Give credit to others, and when you are out on the field, you should
>only think about 2 things: Take it one play at a time, and always think
>first downs.  Good Luck, Ryan.
>-----Drew Brees
>
```

FIGURE 5.1   **Email from Drew Brees**

It was an act of generosity for Brees to respond to an email from a nobody freshman at another university. But the advice he gave me was rich, and I took it to heart as I navigated my own college playing career.

In 2005, I got my first "real job." I had just graduated from Ohio University. After spending my collegiate years focused almost exclusively on football and becoming a professional quarterback, I didn't have a lot to offer off the field yet: I had not networked with a business professional before and had never had an internship. Fortunately, I was hired by a family friend for a telephonic sales role. If I wanted to learn from the experience of a mentor, I needed to ask for it. If I wanted to know how to succeed like the top 10 sales professionals in the company, I would need to reach out to each one and ask them how they'd done it. If I was going to win the business of a customer after a long sales call, I would have to ask for the order.

That tactic of asking never stopped being useful. As my career progressed and I found myself wanting the opportunity to interview for a promotion, I had to speak up and ask for the job. When I decided to start a podcast from scratch with no platform, I knew I would be asking guests to be on a show that did not yet exist. I had no choice: I had to ask. What's the worst that can happen if you ask? You get ignored? They say no? How is that a worse outcome than if you don't ask at all?

Ask. Always.

A TALE OF TWO COACHES

From 1980 to 1982 Ron Ullery was an assistant coach at Centerville High School. His job at the time was to coach the running backs and quarterbacks. About midway through the 1982 season, Coach Ullery's boss had a new plan in mind for him. "Coaching offensive line is too much for me as the head coach," said head coach Bob Gregg. "It's our most important position. You're going to coach the offensive line next year."

Coach Ullery had neither coached nor ever played offensive line before. It was the position on the field that he felt the least knowledgeable about and the least prepared to teach to his players. He was apprehensive and more than a little fearful of taking on that responsibility in a program that had won 91 percent of their games over the past eight years. However, having been brought up by a father who taught him to never back down from a challenge, Coach Ullery started planning how he would attack such a monumental task. He would have to educate himself in the strategies, tactics, and techniques of offensive line play, from the very basics on up. He was not about to allow himself to be the weak link on the coaching staff. On top of that, Coach Ullery's teaching ethos was always about helping his players reach whatever their potential might be. Beginning the following season, those players would be the offensive linemen.

As soon as the 1982 season ended, Coach Ullery immediately turned his attention to reading any books or articles about the offensive line positions that he could find. Beyond devouring the resources he could get his hands on, he decided that he would attend any clinic he was able to and would talk to any offensive line coaches willing to spend time with him. Throughout the winter, that is what he did. By the spring, he felt he had built a good foundation of knowledge, but he knew he had a lot more to learn if he was going to be proficient in the small details that separate great offensive linemen from the good ones.

In 1983, one of the most highly respected offensive line coaches at any level was working his craft just an hour or so's drive south of Coach Ullery. At the time, the Cincinnati Bengals had an outstanding offensive line, which included four-time Pro Bowler Max Montoya and future Hall of Famer Anthony Muñoz. If anyone knew how to coach excellent offensive line play, it was Jim McNally, the Bengals' offensive line coach.

If he could get to talk to Coach McNally, Coach Ullery knew he would learn a ton. He also knew that calling the Bengals offices and asking if he could talk to Coach McNally was a long shot at best. But Coach Ullery figured, the worst thing that could happen was that they would say no. All in all, the risks were low, and his expectations were even lower, but the potential payoff was high. Coach Ullery picked up the phone and dialed the Cincinnati Bengals team offices.

A receptionist answered and asked how she could be of help.

"Could I please speak with Coach McNally?"

"I'm sorry, but Coach McNally is unavailable at the moment. May I take a message?"

"Yes, thank you. My name is Ron Ullery, and I'm a coach at Centerville High School near Dayton. I would like to talk to him about coaching offensive linemen."

When the receptionist responded, her tone of voice had suddenly and drastically changed. "Centerville High School? Do you by chance know Stevie Bachman?"

Coach Ullery could hardly believe his ears. "Yes, I know Steve. He's in one of my math classes."

"Oh, my goodness," the receptionist exclaimed, "I used to babysit Stevie for years when he was a little guy. Hold on a minute. Let me get

Coach McNally for you." She put Coach McNally on the phone, and he invited Coach Ullery to his office at Riverfront Stadium to talk shop about coaching offense linemen in person.

On the appointed day and after school let out, Coach Ullery drove down I-75 to the stadium. Coach McNally was seated behind his desk when Coach Ullery was ushered into the office. Immediately, he noticed that Coach McNally was sporting a full-length cast on one of his legs. He had recently had extensive surgery. After a brief exchange of pleasantries, Coach McNally asked how he could be of help. Coach Ullery answered that he was taking on a new position and explained his limited knowledge of offensive line play.

"Let's get started then. Show me your stance," ordered Coach McNally.

Coach Ullery proceeded to get out of his chair and down into what he thought was a good stance.

"That's not a stance." Coach McNally was in full coach mode as he began teaching Coach Ullery a lesson in the fundamentals. "What position are you playing?' he asked. "How big are you? Are you on the right or left side? Is it a run or pass play? Where are the defenders aligned? How good is the defender? How good are you?" Coach McNally hit Coach Ullery with question after question, all aimed at the myriad of important details that factor into that most basic skill for an offensive lineman: getting in a stance.

For the next *four hours* Coach McNally, a man at the absolute apex of his profession, taught Coach Ullery as if he were a prized rookie offensive tackle. The hobbled pro demonstrated the proper techniques for Coach Ullery even with his leg immobilized in a cast. The two coaches then watched game film through which Coach McNally showed Coach Ullery the tiniest of technical details of offensive line play. At times, the two men were literally firing out of their stance and into blocking position, hitting office chairs at full speed. By the time it was over, Coach Ullery was dripping with sweat and loving every minute of it. When the meeting was over and Coach Ullery was leaving, Coach McNally asked, "Oh . . . are you a Reds fan? If so, they've got a home game tonight. Go through the door at the end of the hallway and take a left. You'll be in the stands. Stay and watch if you want." And with that generous offer, Coach Ullery, the lifelong Cincinnati Reds fan, capped off an extraordinary day with the unexpected treat of watching his favorite baseball team.

Many years later, Coach Ullery would be my offensive coordinator at Centerville, and he remains a mentor and friend to this day. After he shared that incredible story with me, he said, "To this day, after 45 years of coaching high school football, those four hours were the most beneficial learning experience I've had to help me in the coaching profession. Not just because it helped me learn about the offensive line position and the techniques and details that allow you to be successful as a player at this position, of which I had very little previous knowledge. But even more because of how it taught me the importance of the little things. The details, none too small to be unimportant, that are really what make the big things even remotely attainable."

Those four hours were a life-altering experience that continues to leave an impact on him. Through Coach Ullery's own coaching and teaching, Coach McNally's generosity continues to impact countless others, myself included. And none of it would have happened—not the unbelievable turn of events that day in 1983, not any of the future impact, *none of it*—without Coach Ullery's decision to pick up the phone and ask for help.

STACK THE DECK

Maria Konnikova is a bestselling author and award-winning journalist who has a PhD in psychology from Columbia University. Despite all her previous success in the world of journalism, teaching, and writing, she wanted to conquer something she'd never done before. Maria wanted to play against the best poker players in the world, and she wanted to *beat them*. Her doctoral work was on risk and emotional decision-making in uncertain environments. According to Konnikova, these are "the precise sorts of conditions you encounter at the poker table."[5] Her theoretical findings, alongside her new practical experience, provide insight into the human decision-making process in environments far removed from the poker table.

When Maria decided to take aim at excellence at the professional poker table, she set out to find the ideal coach. After conducting her research and asking questions of members of the poker community, she identified the coach with whom she wanted to work: Erik Seidel. Known in the poker world as the "Silent Assassin," Seidel is easily one of the best players on the live tournament circuit. Along with his total poker earnings in excess of $37.7 million,[6] Erik's résumé proves he is among the poker elite: he's won eight World Series of Poker titles and has been elected to the WSOP Poker Hall of Fame. Despite his success, Seidel projects a calm and demure demeanor and typically shuns the spotlight. As a result, he doesn't get nearly as much attention from the media as some of his fellow players. But for Maria, that meant Seidel checked all the boxes as being the perfect teacher for her. "There's no one like him," she told me. "He's stood the test of time. He's been successful at poker for decades. . . . He's evolved with the changes of the game, adjusted, and has won. He's kind and humble."

Identifying a best-in-the-profession performer to be your mentor is one thing; finding a way to initiate a relationship that can become a mentorship is quite another. Why would Erik Seidel take Maria on as a student? "It's not for money or exposure. Seidel is notoriously reticent, and he hates sharing his tactics," Maria explained. "I was, however, an ideal pupil in a few ways. Most important, I have a PhD in psychology, and so I was well positioned to understand Seidel's style of play. I also never had much of an interest in cards, meaning Seidel wouldn't have to rid me of any bad habits. My academic training and my inexperience made me a perfect vehicle for an experiment to see if Seidel's psychological game could still triumph over a strictly mathematical style."

Maria's days soon became all about getting better at poker: "studying, playing, living, breathing poker for eight to nine hours a day, every day. . . . Reading, watching videos, or livestreaming very good players."

The results soon followed: Maria went from a novice who had never played poker to winning multiple tournaments and earning over $300,000 in just three years.

Maria's extraordinary results were a direct consequence of her ability to convince Seidel to mentor her. When I asked her how she convinced him to be her coach, Maria gave me a master class on how to ask a busy, successful, introverted person to be your mentor. Here are Maria Konnikova's keys to getting an excellent mentor:

- **Do your homework** and read everything there is to know about the person before contacting them.
- **Be specific** with your ask.
- **Know why** this person should be your mentor.
- Figure out **what's in it for them**.
- Find someone who can help **amplify your strengths**.
- **Get to the point quickly**, and don't write a novel in that first email or DM contact.
- An opportunity to **meet in person** is *always* the best option.
- *Never* say "Can I pick your brain?" Instead, **ask a specific question** so that they can prepare an answer for you.

HOW TO ASK

Whether you are asking for a mentoring relationship or a promotion, the principles underlying a successful ask are the same, according to Alexandra Carter, Clinical Professor of Law and Director of the Mediation Clinic at Columbia Law School. Alexandra teaches people how to become better negotiators. When it comes to asking for something from your employer—whether it is a raise, a promotion, or just additional responsibility—your odds of success are greater if your ask has three key components: it should be optimistic, specific, and justifiable.[7]

When Jeff Immelt started his career at GE in 1982, his first assignment was as a district sales manager in the Plastics Division. The

Dallas, Texas, office he managed sold a product called Noryl, which consisted of little pellets of plastic that businesses used as a base material to mold into instrument panels or car bumpers or hundreds of other products. After getting settled into his role and gaining a firm grasp of the dynamics of the business for which he was responsible, Immelt learned about a tax-free zone in Mexico where people were building factories and warehouse facilities. This gave Immelt an idea, which he pitched to his boss. Customers were frustrated by the time it took GE to deliver their products, Immelt explained to his boss. Believing he could solve this problem by warehousing inventory nearby in Mexico, Immelt said to his boss, "If you give me $45,000 to buy a warehouse down there, and let me stock it, I will lose fewer orders." He got his approval, and his district never lost an order again.[8]

Jeff Immelt understood that he needed to share his vision with optimism, make a very specific ask that could be easily understood and decided upon, and justify his ask by explaining the benefits to his customers (and thus to the company at large and his boss as well). "I need $45,000, and we won't lose orders if you give it to me." Over the course of Immelt's career, a series of moves like this ultimately led him to the role of CEO of GE. The legendary GE CEO Jack Welch chose Immelt to succeed him when Welch retired.

It isn't enough to be known as someone who can identify opportunities. You must be able to consistently make a justifiable ask. Helping those around you understand what you plan to do and how it will be mutually beneficial will increase your odds of receiving what you want. It will be fruitless to make demands of your boss, your peers, or your team without first proving your value to them. Think about your current role and the obstacles in your path. What are creative ways to move through those obstacles and be stronger on the other side? How can you ask for what you want and need with optimism, specificity, and from a justifiable position? Refer to the value you have added in the past and spell out with specificity how you will do that in the future, and your audience is more likely to respond favorably to your ask.

THE UNKNOWN UNKNOWNS

People are notoriously incapable of accurately evaluating their own levels of competency. This cognitive bias was first identified by psychologists David Dunning and Justin Kruger in a 1999 study and came to be popularly known as the Dunning-Kruger effect. It describes the propensity of people with lower-than-average ability at a given task to overestimate their ability at that task. Their research involved studies assessing participants' actual and perceived abilities in humor, grammar, and logical reasoning. Their paper, titled "Unskilled and Unaware of It: How Difficulties in Recognizing One's Own Incompetence Lead to Inflated Self-Assessments," described how across domains, the least skilled are often the most overconfident (see Figure 5.2).[9]

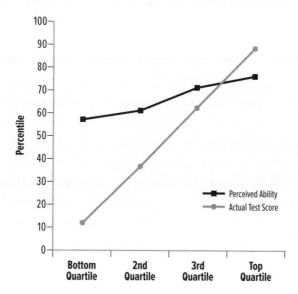

FIGURE 5.2   **The Dunning-Kruger effect**

Everyone has had that know-it-all boss or coworker who actually knew very little. These people hurt team dynamics, stunt growth, and can pull a team's performance down to mediocre (or worse) levels. That said, it's important to note that the Dunning-Kruger effect impacts everyone, including you and me. No one can claim expertise in all domains. Just because you were good at one job doesn't automatically qualify you to be the master of another. In fact, it can have the opposite effect.

A surefire way to fall victim to the Dunning-Kruger effect is to confuse luck with skill. Author, entrepreneur, and marketing professor Scott Galloway understands the difference between the two. Galloway is keenly aware and quite vocal about the role of luck in his success. "The biggest factor in my success was I was born a heterosexual white male in 1964, which meant that I came of age in California where the vision of the regents of the University of California and California taxpayers gave me an amazing undergraduate education at UCLA and then a graduate education at Berkley. . . . I was unremarkable, and yet they had the bandwidth and the admittance capacity to let in an unremarkable kid. . . . I took the SAT three times, and scored in the 80th percentile, which wouldn't get you into a second-tier school now, much less a top-tier school like UCLA. . . . I came into college in the 80s and got an undergraduate and graduate degree for a total tuition of $7,000."

From Scott's perspective, his luck didn't stop there. He went on to describe the circumstances he happened to find himself in that resulted in his trajectory of professional success. "I think there's a virus that plagues a lot of people—I find especially in tech, especially in white males—this virus that infects us is that we conflate luck with talent."[10]

While it's easy for us to think of that bad boss who obviously suffered from this, it's important to know that this impacts us as well. What are some ways we can avoid this?

▶ **Your *who*.** Intentionally surround yourself with those who are willing and able to tell you the truth, even when it's hard. *Especially when it's hard.* This is the steady drumbeat of pursuing excellence. Whom you surround yourself with has as big of an impact as any other action you can take.

- **Be still.** Take a moment to think. Pause. Don't feel forced to make snap decisions and react emotionally during a conversation.

- **Be coachable.** Be grateful for those who are willing to challenge you and give feedback. Prepare yourself to take it and not immediately react defensively or try to argue. They won't always be right, but I've yet to meet a person who doesn't need coaching. Create the space for someone to help you.

- **Question yourself.** Regularly take moments to examine your own assumptions and beliefs. Try to examine all sides of an issue or challenge with the possibility that you may prove your original viewpoint to be wrong. Why do you think what you think? How could you be wrong? What would someone who disagrees with you think? Why would they think what they think?

- **"I don't know."** Don't be afraid to admit it. We all know people who always insist that they know even when they don't. Don't be that person. If you don't know, say it. It's OK. It builds credibility for when you do know what you're talking about.

THE FULL 360

One of the core exercises I do with clients to help them avoid falling into the Dunning-Kruger trap is leading them through a 360-degree review. A 360 review is designed to gather specific feedback from employees above (boss, senior leaders), beside (peers), and below (direct reports).

When I work with clients, I interview coworkers from the three buckets (above, beside, below) and ask them a series of questions to get a full view of the person's strengths and weaknesses. One question that I always ask is an offshoot of the "Start, Stop, Continue" exercise that I've run with teams I've led in the past. I ask, "What is something your colleague should start doing? What is something they should stop doing? What is something they should continue doing?"

There is an art to getting people to open up and share what they truly think. As I listen to what people are telling me, I'm also monitoring their nonverbal cues for indications that they are fearful of being fully transparent. When I detect this, I make a particular note of it to share with the leader I'm working with as evidence of the leader's need to work on creating an environment of psychological safety. If team members don't feel like they can tell me the truth, that is a red flag. I then transcribe the interviews and organize the report to make it easier to digest.

Jack Zenger and Joseph Folkman are two of the premier leadership consultants in the world. The 360 review is a big part of their advising practice when working with clients. According to Zenger and Folkman, here are some of the keys to performing an effective 360 review:[11]

▶ The leader helps choose who among their colleagues should respond to the survey.
▶ The leader personally communicates with those respondents, asking them to provide their candid observations.
▶ The report is presented to the leader, either in a group setting (if multiple people are taking the instrument at the same time) or in a one-on-one coaching conversation.
▶ The leader is provided with context and guidance to understand the data.
▶ The leader also receives a customized set of developmental recommendations, mapped to the company's leadership competencies, to help them create a personal development plan.
▶ There is follow-up from the talent professionals to ensure accountability.

Finally, the most crucial step: take action. It is critical that leaders can not only receive the feedback (positive and negative) but then act on what they just learned. Not following through on the advice given by the members of your 360 is a quick way to lose trust.

I encourage you to go through at least one 360 review a year. It will expand your self-awareness, remind you of past themes you've heard before but forgotten, and ultimately impact your performance. Enlist the help of a professional you trust and do the necessary work to learn.

LISTEN TO COMPREHEND

A prerequisite for any system of feedback to work is the proper approach to listening. For the first Personal Excellence workshop I hosted, I focused on helping attendees become better public speakers. I reached out to a friend of mine who makes his living through improv comedy, both by performing it and teaching others how to do it. I gave him free rein to employ whatever activities he wanted with one caveat: the focus had to be on helping attendees become better communicators. What did we spend the bulk of our time doing? Listening exercises.

Why? In a study of over 8,000 people employed in businesses, hospitals, universities, the military, and government agencies, researchers found that virtually all the respondents believe that they communicate as effectively or more effectively than their coworkers. However, research shows that the average person listens at only about 25 percent of efficiency. While most people agree that listening effectively is an important skill, they don't feel a strong need to improve their own skill level.[12] Cornell Professor Judi Brownell likes to talk about the LAW of listening, which is "Listening = Ability + Willingness. Although listening is a skill you can develop, nothing matters if you don't have a willingness to listen or an interest in focusing and making your listening skill a priority."[13]

Kevin Sharer was raised in California, the son of an aviator father who pushed Kevin to put himself in leadership positions. After earning a master's degree in aeronautical engineering from the US Naval Postgraduate School, Kevin became the construction engineer officer on the *USS Memphis*, a Los Angeles class nuclear submarine. At one point in his career, Kevin took his leadership team to an off-site meeting where he invited the CEO of IBM, Sam Palmisano, to speak to them about leadership. One of Kevin's executive leaders asked Sam why his experience working in Japan was important to his leadership development. Sam said, "Because I learned to listen." He added, "I learned to listen by having only one objective: comprehension. I was only trying to understand what the person was trying to convey to me. I wasn't listening to critique or object or convince."

In that moment Kevin realized that he had spent his career listening with the intention of "waiting to talk." It's something most of us do. We listen with judgment. What Kevin learned that day transformed his future interactions with his team, and instead of short-circuiting the listening process or "waiting to talk," he became an active listener with the intent to understand and comprehend first, before all else. Kevin eventually went on to become the CEO of Amgen, helping sales grow from $1 billion to $15 billion over his 20 years with the company. In 2012, he joined the faculty of Harvard Business School, where he teaches a wide variety of courses in strategy and management. When I spoke with him about his career trajectory, he pointed to that one pivotal moment when he realized he was a poor listener and did something about it.

LEARNING AS A COMPETITIVE ADVANTAGE

In October 2019, I received a text message from one of my literary heroes, Daniel Coyle, author of *The Culture Code* and *The Talent Code.* He asked if I would meet with the senior leadership team of the Cleveland Indians.[14] A few months later, I found myself in a room in Progressive Field, the home of the Indians. Seated around the table with Dan was the team president, Chris Antonetti, and the team's two leaders of learning and development, Jay Hennessey and Josh Gibson.

Before becoming the team's vice president of learning and development, Jay Hennessey spent 25 years serving the United States as a Navy SEAL. He completed numerous deployments all over the world inside and outside the theater of war. In addition to his time abroad, he was involved in the selection and training of young men to become Navy SEALs and Special Warfare Combatant Crewmen. In my conversations with Jay leading up to this meeting, I learned about the importance of humility and curiosity. "Humility is the enabler for curiosity," Jay told me. "It's the enabler for giving praise and gratitude to someone else. Not having to be the center of attention. People without humility don't want to change their mind, or think ideas aren't as good if they aren't their own. . . . Curiosity is an attribute we want from people. But it's easy when you're a 21-year-old ensign. The 21-year-old is curious all day long because he doesn't know anything. But when you're 26 years in the Navy as a Master Chief, can you stay curious? Can you ask your staff, 'What am I missing?' Not everybody can do that. A lot of people get to a level in their career where they think they have it figured out. That can be debilitating for a leader."[15] Having the humility to open your mind, listen, and not having to be the "Chief Answer Executive" because of your leadership title is critical to your long-term improvement and effectiveness.

As our conversation in the conference room at Progressive Field unfolded, Jay and Josh shared how the team valued the building of what they referred to as a learning organization: "We view having a learning organization as a competitive advantage. We're looking to have a competitive advantage where others aren't. When you go back to this idea of great teams, if you break down great teams . . . The team is learning. And it's not just learning to learn. We know if we keep doing what we're doing today, in five years, we're going to be irrelevant. You have to learn as things are growing. For the individual, nobody wants to stay stagnant. The people we hire are passionate, curious people. They want to be best in industry, whatever they are doing. So we have to give them the tools and opportunities for their personal growth and development that makes that team better."[16]

The proof of the benefits of their approach is well documented. Even though Cleveland's player payroll ($37.6 million in 2020) was a fraction of big market teams like the New York Yankees ($110.9 million) and Los Angeles Dodgers ($105.7 million), the Indians could still compete and win. The Indians have succeeded in making the playoffs four out of the last five seasons, including an American League championship run in 2016 that saw them come ever so close to their first World Series win since 1948: they lost by a single run to the Chicago Cubs in an epic extra innings Game 7.

A key part of the Indians' learning organization culture is their monthly TEAMS calls. They invite a wide variety of leaders from both inside and outside the sporting world to participate in a large group Zoom call. There is one designated speaker to kick off the call, and it's typically an author or thought leader on a specific topic. In the second half of the call, attendees go into breakout rooms where each person is asked to share their point of view about that topic. In the instructions email sent to every invitee prior to each call, Jay Hennessey states, "The speaker series is built around learning from our guest speaker and then cultivating dialogue amongst the group. **We ask that those who attend are ready to engage and discuss with others during the session. If you are unable to actively engage, we ask that you wait to view the recording that we will send the following week. Thank you.**" (The boldfacing is Jay's.)

They've learned that learning is done through dialogue. This comes from the work of Peter Senge in his book, *The Fifth Discipline*: "The discipline of team learning starts with 'dialogue,' the capacity of members of a team to suspend assumptions and enter into a genuine thinking together. To the Greeks, *dia-logos* meant a free flowing of meaning through a group, allowing the group to discover the insights not attainable individually."[17]

When building the culture of a team and/or organization, the challenge is creating an environment where there is healthy dialogue and discourse. This can be done with any group of people in any setting: in the corporate world, with sports teams, or even at home. It just requires a commitment to the humility of asking for help and learning from others. Encourage each other to show up prepared to share their point of view because learning happens through dialogue.

6

THE CONFIDENCE FLEX

A master in the art of living draws no sharp distinction
between his work and his play; his labor and his leisure;
his mind and his body; his education and his recreation.
He hardly knows which is which. He simply pursues his
vision of excellence through whatever he is doing, and
leaves others to determine whether he is working or playing.
To himself, he always appears to be doing both.
—LAWRENCE PEARSALL JACKS

Every Sunday morning, I go to a park near my home about 30 minutes prior to sunrise. My purpose is to move my body, and it happens in a very specific order: I run, sprint, and walk. I start with a roughly one-mile run around the loop of the park. Following that, I go onto the grassy field and run a series of 110-yard sprints. Those sprints mirror the conditioning test that we did while I was at Ohio University. Finally, I finish by walking five miles around the neighborhoods near my home.

I often see the same people out there who have their own routines (typically walking the loop around the park). Most weeks for about six months, I would see an older woman walking with her husband. We would nod to each other, say "Good morning," and go about our business. One day, this woman walked up to me as I was cooling down from my sprints and asked, "Why do you run before you walk? Are there health benefits to it?" I could tell that she was genuinely curious. Without thinking and still out of breath from the sprints, I said, "I just try to do the hard stuff first." After I had a moment to catch my breath and think about the interaction, I considered other areas of my life in which I "like to do the hard stuff first" and wondered why I instinctively responded to this woman like that.

I realized that I love the feeling of accomplishing a hard task immediately upon waking up. For me, this is usually something physical. But it is not just limited to that. For example, if I'm in the book-writing process, I try to get some words on the page immediately upon waking up, before much of the day has had time to pass me by.

Also, I want to be able to enjoy my walk. I don't really consider my walk as exercise. It's more of a meditative activity for me. It's time to relax, think, and enjoy being in nature. In fact, researchers at Stanford University have found that walking boosts creative inspiration. By examining the levels of creativity people exhibit while walking versus while sitting, they found that a person's creative output increased by an average of 60 percent when walking.[1] There's more: "Walking on a regular basis promotes new connections between brain cells, staves off the usual withering of brain tissue that comes with age, increases the volume of the hippocampus (a brain region crucial for memory), and elevates levels of molecules that both stimulate the growth of new neurons and transmit messages between them. Because we don't have to devote much conscious effort to the act of walking, our attention is free to wander—to overlay the world before us with a parade of images from the mind's theater. This is precisely the kind of mental state that studies have linked to innovative ideas and strokes of insight," writes Ferris Jabr.[2]

My walk is much more enjoyable after the hard work is complete. I have a sense of accomplishment and an "I-earned-this" feeling. That opens my mind to wander. This frees me to come up with ideas, to stop occasionally to type a note into my phone, and to enjoy the time to myself. Whether it's a physical workout or a mentally taxing project (like writing a book), doing the hardest part first creates momentum.

It's a lot like sledding. It's painful and taxing to trudge up the hill in your snow boots, carrying a sled. It takes effort to get to the top. But once you complete the hardest task, the rest feels much more enjoyable. It's a downhill slide instead of an uphill climb. Ask yourself: if you did those two things in reverse order, would you ever climb up the hill at all?

Map your days. Plan ahead. What is the one action that you can complete early that will create momentum and a downhill sledding feeling for the rest of the day? Tackle that first, and then progress to the next. Doing so will also build confidence in yourself that you can do what's hard, accomplish it, and keep going.

YOUR MENTAL MUSCLE

One of the key attributes I've witnessed after doing more than 400 interviews with some of the most thoughtful leaders in the world is confidence. Confidence is built through preparation, positive output, and the momentum created from stringing together wins. I'm not talking about people who reek of arrogance or are known for having a big ego. I mean the people who have done the work to build confidence over time.

When discussing how to build confidence, Facebook COO Sheryl Sandberg says: "Confidence and leadership are muscles. You learn to use them, or you learn not to. If you are afraid to speak up at a meeting, every time you force yourself to do it, you get better at it. If you're afraid to take your seat at the table, every time you take your seat at the table and you realize no one tells you to go get back to the back row, you learn to do it."[3]

I have felt most confident after going through the preparatory steps that lead to the result I wanted from my performance, whether it's as a closing keynote speaker at an event, a big sales presentation, a football game against a tough opponent, or a compensation meeting with my boss. For me, it comes from the combination of:

1. Preparation for the moment
2. Execution of my plan
3. Experiencing high performance
4. The result that follows

When that happens, it creates muscle memory for me to draw on the next time I'm challenged or potentially doubting myself. The mindset becomes, "I've done this before. I know how to do this. I will do this." That feeling creates confidence. And that confidence becomes a self-propagating mechanism to continue the cycle.

SASHA FIERCE

Speaking on stage in front of hundreds of highly intelligent people can be scary. To help with this, I've drawn from the feedback I received a few years ago from a previous boss. We had not seen each other in a few years, and he was in the audience of one of my keynotes. This was a boss who had been tough on me, and earning praise from him had been rare. After I finished my talk, he met me near the side of the stage.

"Dude! You *really* brought it. I can tell you made the choice to go for it. Huge props, man." It took me a while to think about what he was trying to say. And as I contemplated what he meant by it, I thought about that choice we all must make before any big moment. Given the fear of looking like a fool in front of a lot of people, it's natural to play it safe and just say the words you need to say and get off the stage, while taking as few risks as possible. But that's the path to forgettable mediocrity. No errors get made, but neither do any memories or value for the audience. Instead, I choose to go for it. Given that I'm a natural introvert, my tendency is to spend time in thought and be on the quieter side. Bringing more attention to myself while standing in the spotlight is not in my DNA. Often, my schoolteachers would send notes home to my parents: "Can you please tell Ryan that he needs to talk in class. He never raises his hand and never says anything. It's a problem."

I've had many conversations with my dad about the nerves and fear that we feel prior to walking on stage to give a keynote to thousands of people. I have been in the audience for many of his big keynote presentations, and the thing that has always struck me is how he brims with confidence. "You look so comfortable on stage with all those people watching you," I once told him. "How do you do that?"

"First," he answered, "it helps to get to the repetitions. Every experience doing it helps you feel better for the next one. So, you have to get the reps. Next, I say a quiet prayer to myself that I will have the energy and enthusiasm that this crowd deserves. This speech is for them. It's about them. I need to show up for them. And then I do something that is counter to what I normally think and feel. I say, 'I'm the baddest dude in this room, and I'm about to put on a show.'"

That over-the-top pronouncement of how he feels about himself helps create more confidence and comfort and that shows up on stage. Hearing him describe his process reminded me of one of the world's great performers, Beyoncé Knowles. Growing up, Beyoncé was painfully shy and felt intimidated when speaking with large groups of people. You would certainly never know that now, watching her perform as one of the most confident and charismatic entertainers in the world. How did she go from nervous insecurity to the very icon of self-assured presence? She famously overcame her nerves by creating an alter ego, Sasha Fierce. She even gave this version of herself top billing with her third studio album in 2008, *I Am . . . Sasha Fierce*. Over time, she began to outgrow this need, and in 2010 she told *Allure* magazine, "I don't need Sasha Fierce anymore because I've grown and now I'm able to merge the two."[4]

At some point, hyped-up self-talk and alter egos are no longer necessary. Through the habit of putting into performance the confidence that must be manufactured from those tools—getting "the reps" as my dad put it—it begins to take root.

A few years ago, I was in Washington, D.C., to give the closing keynote at a conference. There were about 400 people in the audience in a hotel ballroom. I got to the venue early to watch the presenters who were on before my time slot of 2 p.m. I noticed that many of the people in the crowd were looking at their phones while the speaker before me was talking. I inched closer, peering over the shoulders of a few attendees, and saw the familiar sight of football games on their phones. A feeling of dread formed in the pit of my gut.

I pulled out my own phone and texted my dad. "This is terrible," I wrote. "Everyone is watching NFL games, and I'm about to go on stage." I should have seen his response coming because there is nothing else I would have expected him to say in that moment.

"You're the baddest dude in that room. Give maximum effort and bring huge energy to the stage." My dad's words acted as a booster shot of refined confidence. I opened the talk with extra excitement and got the people in the audience out of their chairs and away from their phones. I used humor to attack the very thing I was worried about: the fact that I saw people watching NFL RedZone on their phones as I was preparing to go on stage. And I explained that it was my job to be both informative and entertaining. I told them I would be judging myself by whether I was able to keep their attention away from the games, and almost daring them to do it anyway. And it worked: that went on to be one of my most important keynotes of the year. I have since booked more than a dozen speaking gigs from people who were in the audience that day.

I have to tap into my own inner Sasha Fierce and make the choice to go for it when it's time to go on stage. I may run up the stairs, skip a few steps, and open with a booming voice. Immediately, I dive right into a story, a joke, or some other way to let the audience know, "I'm about to put on a show." That self-talk and the actions that follow help me get to the place I need to be, to properly serve the audience. It's all about them and what they get from the experience. I remind myself each time that my mission for that day is to impact them in three ways: I want to change what they think, I want to change how they feel, and I want to compel them to choose to change their behavior for the better. That doesn't happen without making the conscious choice to bring it each time.

NO DISCOUNTING ALLOWED

Jack Butcher is an idea designer. After spending a decade working in corporate advertising as a graphic designer, he has built a business out of his conceptual design expertise. While interviewing him, I couldn't help but notice his quiet yet knowing confidence. He was neither arrogant nor cocky. He had an easy self-assuredness I rarely see. How had he acquired this level of belief in himself? His answer began with a moment when an experienced mentor had verbally hit him right between the eyes with an admonition that has stuck with Jack ever since. Very early in his career as a graphic designer in the advertising world, Jack had a meeting with this mentor to show his work-in-progress on a project. Prior to revealing his work, Jack said, "This isn't as good as it should be. Can you take that into consideration before you look at it?" His mentor quickly responded, "Then why are you showing it to me? I don't want to see it. If you're going to lead with that, then why are you bringing it to me?"

That lesson has framed Jack's work ever since. As he relayed this story to me, he summarized its wisdom with this simple maxim: "Never discount your work prior to showing it." Understand your work. Know how to properly frame it. And then show it with confidence.

But where to get such confidence? Jack explained, "It made me think about how am I going to defend this work as I present it? What would the worst critic say about this work? How would I respond to that?" To be able to answer those questions from others, you have to embrace the responsibility of ownership. Jack referred to it as "owning the full iteration of the story. If someone asks you a question, you can answer at every level. It's similar to when, back at school, you had to show your work. Don't just show up with the answer. Explain how you got there.... That gives you the confidence to defend anything you're presenting."[5]

Jack learned a valuable lesson about doing his research and being prepared for the big moments in his life. You build confidence in your output when you commit to becoming consciously competent in the input that goes into it. String together moments like this and you start to build the momentum of confidence that propels you to the next challenge. Think about big moments in your life—a big test, an interview, a game, a presentation at work. Your preparation and your performance when the lights are bright are what builds your confidence for the next big moment. Work to put yourself in those situations as often as possible, and be ready when it's time to show your work. Don't discount it. Show up confidently knowing that you put in the work when no one was watching in order to perform when everyone is.

MEET THE MOMENT

Within months of moving into the White House as the newly inaugurated forty-fourth president of the United States, Barack Obama and First Lady Michelle Obama invited an eclectic collection of artists and performers for an event like the White House East Room had never seen before, mixing readings of Shakespeare's *Othello* (by no less than the voice of Darth Vader himself, the great James Earl Jones) with the rhythmic cadences of original spoken word poetry. It was billed as "an evening celebrating poetry, music and the spoken word,"[6] but ultimately came to be known colloquially as the White House Poetry Jam.

One of the artists in attendance was Lin-Manuel Miranda, winner of the previous year's Tony Award for Best Original Score for his music and lyrics from the Broadway hit musical *In the Heights*. He was supposed to perform one of the songs from that show, but he decided to bring something different to what was a once-in-a-lifetime opportunity. Instead, he announced to the crowd, "I'm working on a concept album on the life of somebody that I believe embodies hip-hop: Treasury Secretary Alexander Hamilton." The room filled with the kind of laughter one hears when people aren't quite sure if the funny thing they just heard was a joke or the prelude to an awkward spectacle. "You laugh! But it's true!" he exclaimed, and then proceeded to give a quick thumbnail summary of Alexander Hamilton's life story. Then Lin-Manuel Miranda slipped into character as Vice President Aaron Burr and delivered what would eventually become the opening song of *Hamilton*, the musical that would take the theater world and broader culture by storm six years later. This prototype of an ambitious musical project would go on to win 11 Tony Awards and the Pulitzer Prize for Drama in 2016. And the show has generated more than a billion dollars since its release.

When you watch the video of that moment,[7] you see an artist who seems to be dripping with an incredible amount of performer's confidence. But Miranda describes himself and that performance in very different terms. "If you want to see me at my most afraid, you can watch that video," he said, "because I know that Hamilton is a bad elevator pitch—like 'Rapping founders? What? No!' And I think the audience really thought it was a joke, like 'this is a Schoolhouse Rock thing,' or 'this is an epic rap battles of history' like gag thing. And if you watch the video, my eyes are constantly scanning around because I'm looking for an escape route if this goes sideways, like 'How do I get out of the East Room? Where are all the exits if I bomb in front of the president of the United States?'"[8] Michelle Obama would later write that Miranda's performance that night was "the best piece of art I've ever seen."[9]

When you think about big accomplishments in your life, there is a good chance that they were all preceded by some sort of fear. The difference between Lin-Manuel Miranda and a theater performer you've never heard of is how they choose to handle that fear. His preparation and belief in himself are what enabled him to have the guts to get up in front of the most powerful person on the planet and try something new that had never been performed in public prior to that moment.

When your opportunity arises, will you meet the moment? Will you be prepared to perform at maximum capacity? The daily actions you take leading up to these inflection points will be the difference between making the most of the luck that hits you and not. The old adage rings true: "You don't have to get ready if you stay ready." Staying ready is a daily pursuit. The daily micro actions that compound over time are what prepare you to perform at a high level when it matters most.

ACT WHEN OTHERS ARE SCARED

Of course, it can be hard to even know if such a "moment" is before you: whether it is time to hunker down and weather a passing storm or step out into the wind and harness its momentum. But if you study the most impactful leaders and organizations, you will often find that in times of crisis—when adversity strikes and others look to protect what they have and play defense—these leaders summon their courage to go on offense and get aggressive. Let me give you just one example I personally experienced during our pandemic-devastated year of 2020.

In March 2020, right at the beginning of our country's realization that Covid-19 was going to be a massively disruptive national event, I received an inquiry from the leadership team at Dell. "Ryan, we'd like to hire you to work with our leaders," they said. "We need to invest in them now more than ever." In those early uncertain weeks of the pandemic, it was not an email I expected to receive. Most of what was in my inbox was one notice of event cancellation after another, as clients realized that large groups of people gathering for a conference was not going to be happening anytime soon. And I certainly didn't begrudge these clients their cancellations. I understood the death and destruction caused by the pandemic in 2020 and was sensitive to the fact that a lot of businesses were just trying to keep their doors open.

That said, here was Dell, a high-performing business with lots at stake, taking an aggressive posture while others were not. Over the course of the year, I saw two types of businesses beyond the ones that were just trying to survive: those that aggressively looked to hire top talent and invest in them, and those that feared the uncertain world we were in and cut all development costs for their people. In the long term, we'll see which option was best. When they emailed me in March 2020, Dell's stock price was $28 a share. By December 4, 2020, it closed at $72 a share.

BUILD CHARISMA

One of the qualities people associate with confidence is charisma. Charismatic people have a magnetic effect. They draw people to them and keep their attention. Think about the most charismatic people you know and ask yourself, "What qualities do they exhibit?" I've asked myself this question and taken notes on my observations. Here is what I found:

- **They smile first.** It's contagious.
- **They understand the importance of first impressions.** Once formed, first impressions are hard to reverse. Because of this, charismatic people behave with intention when meeting someone for the first time. They look into your eyes, ask questions that pique your curiosity, genuinely listen to your answers, and respond with an even better follow-up question. They mirror the talking speed of their counterpart and create a feeling of connection quickly. They aren't rushed or looking over the person's shoulder for someone "more important." They make the other person feel like they have all the time in the world. It's hard to connect with someone when they seem rushed.
- **They are fully present.** Olivia Fox Cabane, author of *The Charisma Myth*, writes, "Being present—paying attention to what's going on rather than being caught up in your thoughts—can yield immense rewards. When you exhibit presence, those around you feel listened to, respected, and valued."[10]
- **They don't spread negative gossip.** Instead, they focus on sharing excitement about an idea or a person.
- **They are others focused.** "In the torrid London summer of 1886, William Gladstone was up against Benjamin Disraeli for the post of Prime Minister of the United Kingdom. This was the Victorian era, so whoever won was going to rule half the world. In the very last week before the election, both men happened to take the same young woman out to dinner. Naturally, the

press asked her what impressions the rivals had made. She said, 'After dining with Mr. Gladstone, I thought he was the cleverest person in England. But after dining with Mr. Disraeli, I thought I was the cleverest person in England.' Guess who won the election? It was the man who made others feel intelligent, impressive, and fascinating: Benjamin Disraeli."[11]

Jayson Gaignard, founder of MasterMind Talks, knows how to communicate this focus on others as much as anyone I know. When he attended his first Summit at Sea, a leadership voyage designed to foster creativity and connection, he had a very intentional approach to each initial conversation he had. After meeting someone, Jayson would create a new file in the notes section of his phone. Into that file, Jayson would type the interesting qualities he had learned about the person, the names of their spouse and kids, and what they were most excited about. Each night when he went back to his room, Jayson wrote a thank you note to every person he had met. He was sure to include important details of what they'd discussed, he mentioned the names of the important people in their life, and he gave them all his contact information so they could continue their relationship. To be interesting to others, be interested in others.

▶ **They go beyond surface-level questions quickly.** Charismatic people ask the questions that force the person they are with to think more deeply. They don't play devil's advocate, and they don't immediately share their point of view. They ask questions out of genuine curiosity for the other person. They don't simply "wait for their turn to speak." They are focused on helping their counterparts express their thoughts, feelings, and excitement. Rarely do charismatic people waste time talking about the weather.

▶ **They add humor to the conversation.** They have an innate ability to make others smile and laugh without making it feel like they are delivering a stand-up comedy set. Laughter creates a higher level of comfort for others to connect with you.

These charisma-building actions may come naturally to some, but they can also be learned by anyone. If these ways of interacting with strangers don't feel natural to you and are not an innate part of your personality, don't worry. As the mindset work of Carol Dweck reminds us all: we are not set in stone. If we care to connect with others, with the intention of building genuine relationships, then we can all do this. A life of excellence is built on the foundation of having loving relationships with others. These skills are critical to build in order to do that.

THE VALUE OF ADMIRATION

Knowing that others respect our work and find our contribution useful helps feed into the momentum of confidence that we need to tackle the next big mountain we have to climb. But the line between the innocent appetite for confidence-boosting admiration and the dark side of craving adulation to the point of narcissism is not an easy one to draw. How do we feed the former without succumbing to the latter?

"Why am I doing this?" Rich Diviney thought to himself, as he lay motionless on the sand in full darkness as the cold Pacific surf crashed over him. Between Rich and his goal to become a Navy SEAL was Hell Week, and he was smack in the middle of it. Later asked why he wanted to become a SEAL, Diviney didn't hesitate. "To see if I could be a badass special operator. To prove to myself that I could do it. I think that's why most guys do this. I wanted to be recognized as a part of an elite fraternity. I was motivated by narcissism." Rich continued, "Narcissism is what drives us to take risks, to get noticed, which in turn can help us discover potential we didn't know we had."[12]

I do not in any way believe Rich is a narcissist. There are lots of despicable words that make up the definition of narcissism, and there is nothing despicable about Rich Diviney. Rather, he has taken one element of the definition—a craving for admiration—and labeled it as a motivator for him. Narcissism is clinically recognized as a personality disorder. People who score too high on the scale can be dangerous. In

Rich's book, *The Attributes*, he writes, "Excessive narcissists are rarely loyal—loyalty requires trust and a sense of safety—so their tribes are inherently unstable: Healthy members tend not to stay long, and new ones are let in only when they show the requisite deference. Those who do leave usually suffer a disproportionate amount of wrath from the person to whom they once deferred—because defectors are considered enemies. The energy and effort of the highly narcissistic person will be used to prop up their fragile egos rather than to achieve shared objectives or serve a common purpose."[13]

It's important to understand the delicate balance between suffering from a personality disorder and the beneficial factors of craving admiration as motivation for pursuing excellence. Humans are wired to crave adulation, praise, and rewards. It's in our DNA from our tribal days. If we are recognized for doing something positive for the tribe, the likelihood of keeping our position in the tribe is much higher. One of the biggest issues I've observed is when celebrities or people in a position of power surround themselves with people who only tell them what they want to hear: yes-men or yes-women. This feeds narcissism and can be extremely dangerous. Those types of people will not allow dissenters in their organization. Don't be that person.

As you look at your actions, especially as they relate to others, it is a good practice to continually question yourself to ensure your narcissism balance stays in check. Am I making this too much about me? Do I lash out at others if they no longer want to be on my team? What am I learning from the exit interviews with team members who are leaving my company? What am I doing to be a great friend? How am I there for others? Do I have long-term friendships or a lot of shorter-term acquaintances?

Being willing to hold up a mirror to yourself and really question your thoughts, feelings, and behaviors can be helpful when determining whether your narcissistic tendencies are in check. But alone, these worthwhile efforts are not enough. You have to surround yourself with people who are willing to share the absolute truth with you: those who love you and have the guts to let you know when you are out over your skis. Who have you given *explicit* permission to tell it to you straight when you have crossed the line from charisma to narcissism? How are you playing that role for others? Cultivate and build genuine relationships. Holding each other accountable is part of the love you show for one another.

It's natural to want some adulation and applause. We don't need to lie to ourselves about that. But we need to be aware of it and regularly spend moments reflecting on it. We must stay vigilant if we are to keep ourselves in balance to best serve our families, friends, and colleagues. There is nothing narcissistic about wanting to do great work and achieve the praise and admiration that often comes along with such positive actions.

Living a life of excellence both requires and grows confidence. It's a muscle you can develop by doing the hard stuff first, preparing thoroughly, being willing to risk going big, and taking responsibility of ownership. Foster your own Sasha Fierce to handle the fear that comes with stepping up. Put in the reps of daily action to get ready and stay ready to show up when the moment demands it. Build charisma by focusing on others and use your natural desire for admiration as a motivation. While it's important to be thoughtful and prepared, the greatest confidence is built *through the doing*. Do the work!

PART III

THE CHASE

7

MAKING THE COMMITMENT

It had long since come to my attention that people of
accomplishment rarely sat back and let things happen
to them. They went out and happened to things.
—ATTRIBUTED TO LEONARDO DA VINCI

Marshall Goldsmith, coach to some of the world's most impactful CEOs and author of *What Got You Here Won't Get You There*, says that when considering making a commitment, we all should ask ourselves this question: "Am I willing, at this time, to make the investment required to make a positive difference on this topic?"[1] When Marshall joined me on my podcast, he told me how he uses the willingness to commit to determine which clients he works with and the nature of his relationship with them. To all clients, he makes the same offer: the investment in Marshall is $250,000 per year. Together, he and the client set key metrics and milestones by which to measure success. If they hit them, then Marshall keeps the money. If not, he pays it all back to the client. He is 100 percent committed when he chooses to work with someone, and he puts his money where his mouth is. He told me, "I bet on myself. I don't get paid unless my coaching works." His willingness to commit to his clients is why he is in high demand and charges what he does. And ultimately, his commitment is part of what drives his results. Without the results, he's out of business.[2]

OPPORTUNITY IS NOT A LENGTHY VISITOR

Into the Woods is a Tony Award–winning musical written by Stephen Sondheim that fuses the stories of Cinderella, Little Red Riding Hood, Rapunzel, and Jack and the Beanstalk and explores the consequences of the characters' wishes and desires. As Cinderella visits the grave of her mother, lamenting the futility of her dream to attend the King's festival, she sings: "I've been good, and I've been kind, Mother, doing only what I learned from you. Why then am I left behind, Mother? Is there something more that I should do? What is wrong with me, Mother? Something must be wrong. I wish . . ." And Cinderella's mother responds, "What, child? Specify. Opportunity is not a lengthy visitor, and good fortune, like bad, can befall when least expected."[3]

I was reminded of this line when I interviewed Liz Forkin Bohannon for my podcast.[4] In 2008, Liz moved to Uganda to learn more about the issues facing women and girls living in extreme poverty. While in Africa, she met a group of young women who had tested well enough to gain admittance to college but couldn't afford to go. In response, Liz designed a pair of sandals, set up a manufacturing site, and hired three young women preparing to graduate from high school. To these women Liz made the following promise: that if they made these sandals during the nine-month gap between high school and college, they would earn enough money to attend college. Ten years later, Liz's company, Sseko Designs, is now a women's lifestyle brand with over 300 products, all sourced from ethical, fair-trade manufacturers. They've enabled hundreds of female scholars to go to college and have created jobs for thousands of women all over the world. Liz emphasized that opportunities are there, and it's on us as leaders to fight through our imposter syndrome and be prepared when an opportunity arises to make the most of it without hesitation or fear—what she calls acting with "beginner's pluck"—because *opportunity is not a lengthy visitor.*

We can all recall moments of opportunity in our lives, the biggest of which are often preceded by scary thoughts and strenuous preparation. One such moment for me was when I interviewed for a big promotion. I was a regional sales manager going for the position of "segment director," a title that carried the responsibilities of leading a division of our business. My interview with the hiring vice president could make or break that (potentially) life-changing job. I walked into the room for my interview with him: an intimidatingly intelligent VP (and future CEO).

As I sat down across from him, he pulled out his phone and set it on the table. On its screen I could see the timer app. He said, "You have 30 seconds. What are all the productive things you can do with a rock? Go!" And with that, the timer started. Now, I'm still not entirely certain what he was trying to learn by asking this, but I imagined at the time that he was judging how I would handle a pressure situation. I was not prepared for a question like this. How could I have been? I'd never thought about the production value of a rock before, and certainly not with a person timing me while I did it. I tried my best to calmly list as many useful things as possible: break a window, build a dam, paint it, etc. When my time was up, he said, "That was good!" Immediately following the encouragement, he asked, "How many new homes will be built in the United States next year? You can do the math in your notebook if you want." Seriously? Again, I've never thought about the number of homes built in a year. Again, he was judging my ability to think on my feet and come up with a solution to something I hadn't previously thought about. This was a moment in my career, and I could meet it or not.

If you're reading this book, you are probably the type of person who is regularly looking for opportunities to grow and progress. Your thoughts and behaviors leading up to these moments are what will define your future. As Cinderella's mother told her, "Opportunity is not a lengthy visitor, and good fortune, like bad, can befall when least expected." If you are going to be primed to take advantage of those fleeting opportunities when they arrive, think now about how to prepare yourself each day to be a rigorous thinker, remain calm in times of chaos, and prove to others that you can handle ambiguity. Regularly put yourself in situations in which you're forced to think on your feet and react with rational, useful ideas. Fortunately, I ended up earning that promotion in part because of how I performed in the interview, and my ability to do well came from the practices I had made part of my life long before the interview. As you prepare yourself for the opportunities you do not yet see, here are a few actions to take:

- ▶ **Meet with mentors who are more experienced and wiser than you.** Come prepared to ask questions. Before each meeting, think, "What do I want to learn about today?" Don't go into a meeting wanting to pick someone's brain (and please *never* say that). Go to it with thoughtfulness and intention. Be purposeful and prepared.

- ▶ **Read daily from a wide range of sources.** As startup founder Wes Kao has written, "Develop adjacent skills to make you better in your role. The adjacent disciplines will give you the je ne sais quoi that expands your lateral thinking. They make you sharper, savvier, and more nuanced. The adjacent topics will help you develop your sense of judgment. You'll improve at making high-quality, high-velocity decisions—which will ultimately help you translate your intent into strong execution."[5]

- ▶ **Sign up for challenging events.** Is there a hard project at work that needs doing? Raise your hand. A triathlon? Register and learn how to prepare to accomplish something new. Improv class? Take a friend and get comfortable embarrassing yourself in front of other people. Regularly putting yourself in the position of doing the hard work will better prepare you for the unexpected challenges that inevitably will arise as you progress on your pursuit of excellence.

A SPARKLING POCKET OF GREATNESS

In 1976, Anne Mulcahy started her new job as a field sales rep with the Xerox Corporation. Over the course of the next two decades, Anne steadily moved up the organizational hierarchy, earning one promotion after another. When asked how she did it by leadership scholar Jim Collins, Anne replied, "I tried to make my minibus a sparkling pocket of greatness."[6] In August 2001, 25 years after she first joined the company, the board of directors came to Anne and said, "We want you to drive the whole bus." At the time, Anne would later tell the Families and Work Institute, "To be very honest, this was less like being promoted than it was being drafted into a war because we had some very serious issues." By the time she became the CEO, Xerox was $17.1 billion in debt, its stock was losing value, and bankruptcy seemed a likely outcome. Today, Xerox has been transformed, and Anne Mulcahy is credited with leading the dramatic turnaround during her decade at the helm.[7]

The question of how to get promoted is one I am asked often and one I asked a mentor of mine. Bryan Miller was a vice president and my boss's boss at LexisNexis during my time there as a sales manager. He started with the company as a field sales representative (the same role Anne Mulcahy had when she started at Xerox). Bryan remains one of my favorite leaders, and I'm lucky to call him a friend. I asked him, "How have you been promoted so much over the course of your career?" In his humble yet confident Southern drawl, Bryan said, "Well, Ryan, in reality, I don't think about that. I think about doing my current job in as great a fashion as I can possibly do it. That's my only focus. And it seems that when I've done that, I keep getting tapped on the shoulder for more responsibility." Just like Anne had done at Xerox, Bryan had worked to make his minibus a sparkling pocket of greatness. And that is what has led to his productive and meaningful career.

But, according to Bryan, there's another important part to keep in mind. "Doing your current job really well is a prerequisite. It gets you to the dance. In addition, I tell others to start applying for a role of greater responsibility *before* the role is open. By 'applying' I mean understand the skills/knowledge you will need in the role you desire. If the role you want requires more public speaking than your current role, start developing those skills prior to the role opening to demonstrate your capabilities for the greater responsibility. If the role you want requires

P&L (profit and loss) responsibility (and your current role does not), take courses to get the financial acumen the role will require *before* the role is open. Getting mentors to share what those competencies are and getting human resources partners to share job descriptions/requirements will help with this preparation."

Play the long game. Follow your genuine curiosity when asking questions. Choose a job working for leaders who will level you up by being around them. Look for high-ceiling leaders, those who have not yet reached their peak. Build meaningful relationships with people who have decision-making power within your company as well as outside of it. Most leadership roles are decided long before the interview process starts. This may feel unfair, but high-level executives often hire people they know. They want someone whom they've seen do excellent work for years.

In my case, I met a West Point and Harvard MBA graduate named Lee Rivas early in my career on a "Circle of Excellence" awards trip. The trip was a reward for the top producing sales professionals, giving us the opportunity to mingle in an informal setting at an exotic locale with the company's senior leaders. Lee was one of those leader-hosts, and after hitting it off with him, I asked him if he would be amenable to setting up quarterly calls. He agreed. When the time came for each call, I showed up prepared with specific questions and I took detailed notes. After the calls ended, I typed up my notes, and created an action plan based on the new learnings from Lee. I would write, "Lee—Thank you for your investment in me. Here is what I learned . . . Here is what I intend to do . . . And by the way, feel free to forward this email to anyone else you mentor. Hopefully, it could help others as well." Doing this strengthened my relationship with a high-level leader. Lee knew that I took his advice seriously and worked to implement what I was learning. On top of that, I was trying to help others along the way.

Fast-forward six years from our first encounter. Out of the blue, I received a text message from Lee that said, "Hey, you have a minute? I want to talk with you about an opportunity." I called him. He said, "I'm making a change and want you to be a VP of sales for me. It's a big revenue job, but I think you're ready. What do you think?" Without me even knowing it, the interview process for this job had started over the course of the six years leading up to it. I was trying to make my minibus a sparkling pocket of greatness while building relationships at the same time. I had no intention of ever working with Lee. I simply approached him with curiosity and a desire to learn. And he liked that. When the time came for an important role on his team, he called me. Again, I realize that some people don't appreciate that business can work this way, but it's better to live in reality. People hire people they trust, like, and know.

STAND OUT AND SPEAK UP

For about two years of my time at LexisNexis, I got to work with a leader who exemplified courage, humility, confidence, preparedness, humor, and authenticity. Her name was Dustyn Kim, and she's one of my all-time favorite bosses. During our staff meetings, she didn't shy away from sharing the brutal facts of difficult work missions facing us. At the same time, she would present us with an effective strategy to achieve the goal set before us. Over the time I worked for her, I found Dustyn to be the smartest person in nearly every room she entered. Her commitment to being true to who she is as a person made all of us want to commit to perform at our best for her.

Dustyn grew up with an artist for a mother and a senior technology executive for a father. When she was 15 years old, her dad woke her up one morning with a suit from Ann Taylor in hand. "Get up. We're going to Wall Street, and you're going to intern for the summer." Dustyn initially protested, "No, Dad! I'd rather be a lifeguard or do a fun summer job." Her argument didn't persuade her dad. An hour later, they were on their way to Wall Street. Following her high school days as a Wall Street intern, Dustyn went on to Denison University for her undergraduate degree. Upon graduation, she got a job as a consultant, and then went to Wharton for her MBA. She came to LexisNexis after being recruited from the consulting world, and is now the chief revenue officer at Artsy, an online platform and marketplace for fine art.

I recently recorded a podcast with Dustyn and asked her one of the questions I get asked a lot: What is some advice for people who are younger and want to build an excellent career? Her answer struck me as useful, novel, and true. Dustyn said, "It's really two things: stand out and speak up."[8]

Stand out: "Be great at what you do. Be the best at your role. Put in the time and go the extra mile."

Speak up: "Talk about what you want and where your interests lie. I think a lot of people earlier in their career make the mistake of assuming that because they're great, someone will come to them and offer them the next great role that opens up on the team. And when they don't get it, they come to me and say, 'I'm so disappointed that I wasn't considered for that.' And I always ask, 'Well, did your boss know you were interested in that role?' Think about who it would be good to inform what your career goals are and tell them."

I remember the moment when I called Dustyn to tell her that I was leaving my job as a director in a general management role to become VP of sales at our sister company. I was nervous and felt bad because I loved working with her. She made me so much better. I told her the news and she said, "Wow, I'm excited for you. But I didn't know you wanted to go back into sales. Why didn't you tell me? I could have helped you get a VP of sales role in my organization, and we could continue working together."

At that point, I realized that I had made the mistake of not being clear about what I wanted. I wanted to progress. I wanted to get promoted. I wanted to be a vice president. But I never told her. It was a learning moment for me: I needed to be open about what I wanted, and it would have helped me to tell her long before that phone call informing her that I would be leaving.

When you analyze your career, how are you ensuring that you are excellent at your current role? And are you vividly clear with your boss and the people in your network about what you want? Don't assume that they know. They probably don't. Tell them. Be open. You'll be amazed at the doors that open when you're exceptional at what you do and the people who care about you know what you want. Being exceptional at your current role and being proactive about what you want are the table stakes to excellence in a career.

THE SHAPE OF A LAUGH

Dayton-area writer Jodi Smith describes a surprising moment that happened on a night out. She and her husband were at Wiley's Comedy Club in downtown Dayton's Oregon District when the night's emcee made an announcement that an unscheduled special guest comedian would be taking the stage after the show's headliner finished. To Jodi's shock, the special guest turned out to be "none other than Dave Chappelle," one of the world's best stand-up comics. Chappelle has a home in the small college town of Yellow Springs about a half-hour east of Dayton. Jodi writes that Chappelle had just "stopp[ed] by from his home . . . to workshop some new material and surprise local comedy fans."[9]

Like Jodi, I've been fortunate to be in the audience when Chappelle has shown up to work on his craft in this way, preparing for larger future audiences by flexing his comedic muscles before a small club crowd. Like a lot of excellent comedians, Chappelle views himself as a continuous work in progress. This has become the framework for many of the most productive comedians in the world. Jerry Seinfeld typically spends his day writing in a Manhattan office. Then, instead of going home, he shows up unannounced at a random comedy club in New York or New Jersey and inserts himself in that night's lineup. This is a man who's at the very pinnacle of his profession and with a net worth approaching billions. Yet he still feels compelled to hone his act in situations like this, trying a new line here, working on a new bit there. He analyzes the laughter of the audience. Why do this? "To a guy like me," Seinfeld explains, "a laugh is full of information. The time of it, the shape of it, the length of it—there's so much information in a laugh. A lot of times, you could play me just the laughs from my set, and I could tell you, from the laugh, what the joke was. Because they match."[10]

Long before you ever see a joke on a Netflix comedy special or in a sold-out theater, each humorous anecdote has been cut, carved, and workshopped for years (in some cases) to ensure that it's funny and gets to the point in as few words as possible. The best performers in the world are constantly a work in progress. Comedians Bill Burr, Tiffany Haddish, and Zach Galifianakis have been known to work on material in this way. When asked about the creative process for his dark and very un-PC brand of comedy, Anthony Jeselnik says, "I can't just create this in my bedroom. I have to get out there on stage, and it has to be a constant process. If I'm trying to develop material, I want to do as many shows as I can." And when testing new material on a smaller audience, he has an anything-that-doesn't-get-a-big-laugh-gets-tossed mentality. He explains, "A lot of times I'll think something's great, and the audience says, 'No, no, no. You're wrong.' Maybe I keep trying it for a little bit, but they eventually talk me out of it. It's not fun to bomb with a joke . . . but the only reason I tell a joke at all is for laughs. So, if the crowd can't get on board, then I lose it."[11]

I'm inspired by learning about the process that the funniest people in the world go through to make others laugh. From the outside, it looks like they wander around on stage and just start talking. Yet what we don't realize is that every single word has been carefully thought through and has been rehearsed and stress-tested thousands of times before we hear it.

How does this apply to the rest of us? The path to excellence is the same. We are all a work in progress. Nobody does it perfectly the first time. That CEO who blew you away at your recent town hall meeting? She probably practiced the speech many times to make it that good. The person at work you look up to? They are a work in progress. They make mistakes. They are constantly working through it. We all are. The difference between the ones who are sustaining excellence and those who are not is that they know it's part of the process and they embrace that. They embrace the struggle. They continue in the face of the struggle and learn to love it. It's part of the process. The ones who don't make it? They quit and don't continue because it's hard. Here are some keys to avoid making that same mistake:

- **Experimental mindset.** Look at life as a series of experiments. Be purposeful about stretching your edges.
- **Failure = right path.** In fact, if you aren't failing or stumbling from time to time, then you aren't stretching yourself enough. The excellent stand-up comedians bomb sometimes. It's just part of the process.
- **Study.** Read about the process behind how someone accomplishes something great. You've heard about Kobe Bryant's legendary work ethic? Yes, he was born with talent, but he worked like crazy to always improve. Behind all excellence is typically a framework that you can learn and apply.
- **Bias for action.** Remember what we learned from Herminia Ibarra, "We learn who we are in practice, not in theory." Get on the stage. Do the work. Learn from doing it.

ADAPT LIKE THE FROG

According to the decades of research done by geologists, paleontologists, and biologists around the globe, the world's dinosaurs went extinct roughly 65 million years ago. The evidence buried in the rocks and coded into the fossil record makes clear the drastic change in the Earth's biodiversity along what has come to be known as the K-T boundary: the marker between the Mesozoic Era of the dinosaurs and the Cenozoic Era that followed without them.[12]

A meteorite crashed into the earth along the tip of the Yucatan Peninsula at a site known as the Chicxulub Crater, causing this literal line in the sands of time, frozen in rock. This extinction-level event proved catastrophic for dinosaurs and just about everything else on the planet. Except, it didn't kill *everything*. In the aftermath of the cataclysm, one of the surprising types of animals that not only survived but thrived was frogs. About 9 in 10 frog species today evolved from three frog lineages that survived the event, according to research published in *Proceedings of the National Academy of Science.*[13]

According to David Wake, a herpetologist at the University of California, Berkeley, frogs are nature's "master survivors." While most of the planet's animal life was dying off as the food chain collapsed around them, seed-bearing trees and other flowering plants suddenly dominated the landscape. This changed environment played to the frog's ability to take advantage and begin "experimenting with new ways of life," like living in trees for the first time, says Wake. That skill—adaptability—not only made it possible for frogs to survive the turmoil of the K-T event; it is what fueled the animal's ability to outperform others in the Darwinian race into the future. In fact, many of the new frog species that descended from that surviving trio started laying eggs on land. The offspring of some even took to skipping the tadpole phase altogether and started growing directly into a small frog. What this research shows, Wake says, is that frogs have the proven ability to "take advantage of opportunities—in this case, an ecological vacuum that existed following the mass extinction."[14]

I mentioned previously that I had the good fortune to meet a leader named Lee Rivas, who was, on paper, a 10 out of 10. He graduated from the U.S. Military Academy at West Point, became a tank commander, and then attended Harvard Business School. Upon entering the business world, Lee used what he'd learned from those formative years in the military and at Harvard to great results. Lee quickly rose through the ranks at our company, and I wanted to know how he did it.

"Well, I'm assuming it's because you have a military leadership background combined with an MBA from Harvard?" I said, starting the conversation off by trying to get right to the point.

"That doesn't hurt," he responded, "but those qualifications only get you in the door. Once you get the job, you have to achieve results, regardless of the challenging circumstances you find yourself in. And the key learning that I've taken from the battlefield to the business world is adaptability. The world changes quickly . . . This business changes constantly. You are tasked with selling one product to one set of customers now, but that all can change tomorrow. The people who rise up in this profession are the ones who can adapt and thrive, while others complain about wanting to continue doing what made them successful."

Shifting my mind to expect change and yearn for it, viewing change as an opportunity to distinguish myself in the business, was a game changer for me. As I had more conversations with leaders who had built fantastic careers, they all kept repeating variations on this theme: adaptation was critical because the state of business was in constant flux.

"Every person who has walked through my door has had a problematic relationship with change," writes psychotherapist Julia Samuel, author of *This Too Shall Pass: Stories of Change, Crisis, and Hopeful Beginnings.* "Change is the one certainty of life, and pain is the agent of change, it forces you to wake up and see the world differently, and the discomfort of it forces you to see the reality of it. It's through pain that we learn, personally and universally." Further, it's the acceptance of change and attitude toward it that makes you better prepared to handle it well. Samuel continues, "It's the paradox that the more you allow yourself to accept that change is inevitable, the more likely you are to change intentionally and adapt."[15] When everything around you is transforming in puzzling ways and at a dizzying pace, excellence requires that we position ourselves as master survivors searching enthusiastically for new and better ways to adapt to our changing environment—just like those Mesozoic frogs.

IT STARTS WITH HOW YOU SEE YOURSELF

"If you're always the victim, you'll find that people get tired of carrying your load," Donald Miller told me during his second appearance on my podcast. Don is the founder and CEO of StoryBrand, an organization that helps companies clarify their brand and the messages they use to sell it. In addition to being a highly sought-after marketing savant,

Don is a *New York Times* bestselling author who has worked in the White House with US presidents, has helped award-winning actors and actresses, and has even consulted with Super Bowl–winning NFL coaches. He's spent decades studying the makeup of excellent performers. During our conversation, he shared with me three key differences that separate the achievers of excellence from the rest. For Don, becoming what he calls a "value-driven successful person" all starts with how you see yourself in your own story.

Be the Hero (Not the Victim)

How often do you position yourself as a victim in your own life's narrative? How often do you talk about yourself (whether to others or to yourself mentally) as though you are not in control of your life? Do you believe other people are responsible for your failures?

Don was born in Texas and grew up poor after his father left and never came back. His mom had to work long hours just to keep him and his sister fed and clothed, and even then it wasn't enough. "Mom worked extremely hard, but we still had to stand in line for government cheese. She never made a living wage," he recounted. It would have been easy and even understandable for him to have succumbed to the temptation of a victim mentality. In life, playing the role of victim "helps us out of the responsibility that is ours . . . [and] attracts a rescuer, somebody to come in and do the work for you. . . . The biggest transformation in my life happened when I stopped thinking of myself as a victim and started thinking of myself as the hero," Don told me. He credits the change in his life's trajectory to shifting his thinking and sense of identity to that of a hero mentality. "I lost 150 pounds and became more in control of my life."[16]

Be a Good Investment

"Value-driven successful people are obsessed with getting others a strong return on the investment made in them. People who are obsessed with being a good investment attract further investment and get to enjoy more personal economic value. When you offer greater economic value within the economic ecosystem, you are paid more, given more responsibility and promotions, and are sought after by customers looking for value. In business, your boss may really like you, but in large part, bosses see you as an economic investment. There is nothing wrong with that. So how do we become ridiculously successful? By making other people absurdly successful."[17]

Exhibit a Clear Bias Toward Action

"They don't let ideas die on the vine. They take action to make those ideas happen. While others may have terrific ideas or be able to see an important issue from many angles, action-oriented people are good at getting things done." People who view themselves as a product or service to better the lives of others increase their odds of achieving the outcomes that they want. Having an others-focused approach to life and work means asking yourself some tough questions: How do you add value to your boss's life? How do you add value to the lives of your clients? Here's a great exercise you can do right now: Take out a sheet of paper and write down specifically how you improve the lives of people in your professional life. Do the same exercise for your personal life. Now comes the hard part: What purposeful actions are you prepared to take to help others who are important to you?

This bias for action is all about taking the initiative and following through to completion. It's a quality in high demand by employers like Jake Wood who are looking for excellence. Jake is a Marine Corps combat veteran of Iraq and Afghanistan and the CEO of Team Rubicon. Over the past two decades, he has navigated the world's most complex environments, whether disaster zones, humanitarian crises, battlefields, or startup boardrooms. His organization has become one of the fastest-growing nonprofits in America and is celebrated for its unique culture, innovation, and impact. When I asked him what he looks for when making a hiring decision, he told me, "You have to take initiative—but initiative doesn't matter if you crumble at the first sign of opposition, so you need tenacity to overcome anything that gets in your way. Finally, if you can't do it with an infectious level of enthusiasm and no one wants to be around you, you're not worth having on the team."[18]

When considering who to be around as you're striving for excellence, whether in business or in life, think about what they bring to the table. Do they act with the initiative and willingness to be proactive that comes from a hero mentality? Or do they sit back and wait to be told what to do, a classic victim mentality tell? Are they the kind of person who "goes beyond the spec," as Seth Godin would say?[19]

And what type of energy are *you* bringing to the team? By regularly bringing positive energy, optimism, and enthusiasm, you can help propel others to achieve levels of excellence they wouldn't otherwise. My dad always told me, "It is your duty as the leader to be in a good mood for your team every day." Be the type of person who brings a contagious smile and enthusiasm to the room. That is the type of person I want on my team.

8

BUILDING YOUR BAND

*If you're not in the arena also getting your ass kicked, I'm not
interested in your feedback. If you have constructive feedback
you want to give me, I want it ... But if you're in the cheap seats,
not putting yourself on the line, and just talking about how I
can do it better, I'm in no way interested in your feedback.*

—BRENÉ BROWN

Jeni Britton Bauer is an ice cream pioneer. In 2002, she founded Jeni's
Splendid Ice Creams upon her uniquely "modern, ingredient-driven
style of ice cream making" that sparked the now trendy artisanal ice
cream movement. *Food and Wine* magazine wrote "No one else makes
ice cream like Jeni Britton Bauer." *Fast Company* described Jeni as "one
of the most creative people in business today,"[1] and the Aspen Institute
named Jeni to its twenty-first class of Henry Crown Fellowship leaders in 2017.[2] Her first ice cream cookbook, *Jeni's Splendid Ice Creams
at Home*, was a *New York Times* bestseller, earning the moniker the
"homemade-ice-cream-making Bible" from the *Wall Street Journal* and
winning the 2012 James Beard Award for excellence in culinary writing.

Jeni and her brand of ice cream excellence call Columbus, Ohio,
home, just a 90-minute drive from me. I was able to interview Jeni in
person for her appearance on my podcast. As we sat together in front
of a live audience, I had to ask her for the secret to her success. How did
she go from where she started 20 years ago to being recognized as the

industry leader, with her ice cream sold nationwide in stores like Whole Foods and in Jeni's Scoop Shops in 14 major cities across the country? I expected to hear about the value of using all natural, locally sourced ingredients, or about the need for a focused brand identity. While those are, of course, important to the success of Jeni's Splendid Ice Creams, that's not what we discussed. Instead, she talked about connecting with people: you have to "create a craveable reason to return."

"If we create a community, everything falls into place. Put your values front and center and merge with the community. When the community sees your business as vital, they will help you when times are tough," Jeni told us.[3] She knows from experience. When a single pint of Jeni's ice cream in the market tested positive for listeria, the company didn't hesitate. Without waiting to see if an outbreak occurred (it never did), they recalled six months' worth of product, destroying 265 tons of ice cream. The company took a loss of $2.5 million, which almost put her out of business at the time. For Jeni, this costly act of proactive sacrifice was necessary, neither because the product was proven to be contaminated nor because the FDA ordered the recall. It was simply a matter of caring for the Jeni's Splendid Ice Creams community. "There's nothing more important, whether in the financial industry or ice cream, than trust."

"Why would a customer come back to you? Why would someone follow you?" Jeni asked us all rhetorically. "What are you doing as a leader that makes someone want to follow you?" Jeni isn't merely in the business of selling ice cream. She is in the excellence business, and how she views her responsibility to other people is as important to that business as the milk Jeni buys from local dairy farmers.

You need to create a craveable reason to return.

That statement stuck with me all night after talking with Jeni. We all should strive to create a craveable reason to return, regardless of our industry, profession, or goals. Think: Does my behavior make other people want to continue having me in their lives? Are my actions making the lives of others better? Am I delivering value to the greater community?

Pursuing excellence is a team sport. Am I conducting myself in a way that gives others a craveable reason to work with me again? To be in a relationship with me? To entrust me with their business? To pay me their attention as a listener? To give me their time as reader? If the answer isn't yes, then whatever level of good I think I am achieving with my efforts, it is not excellence.

MAKE TRUST YOUR OPENING BID

Jim Collins has written some of the most iconic leadership books of our time. *Good to Great* was the first leadership book I ever read, and I loved *Great by Choice. Beyond Entrepreneurship 2.0* was special for Jim; it was a project he coauthored with his late mentor, Bill Lazier. Bill had been one of the first adults to take an interest in Jim's work many years ago. As mentors often do, Bill went to bat for Jim on many occasions. It was Bill who worked to convince the Stanford Graduate School of Business to hire Jim to teach an entrepreneurship class to Stanford MBAs when he was just 30 years old.

It was the good fortune of pure happenstance that Jim's and Bill's paths crossed. At the time, Lazier was a successful entrepreneur in his fifties who had been asked by the academic dean at the Stanford Graduate School of Business to join the faculty and teach an elective course. Collins, then a not-yet-25-year-old student, had tried to enroll in a different elective course. But thanks to the random lottery system that apportioned class assignments, Jim ended up in Bill's first-ever class. From this grew a relationship that changed the course of Jim's life. As he put it during a recent conversation, connecting with Bill Lazier under those circumstances was like being "hit with a lightning bolt of 'WHO' luck." ("Who" luck, according to Jim Collins, is when you come across somebody who changes your trajectory or invests in you, bets on you, or gives you guidance and key points.)

One of the most impactful qualities about Bill Lazier that forever shaped Jim's view of excellence arose out of a discussion the two men were having about trust. Jim said, "Bill, the truth is not all people are trustworthy. I've been burned. Haven't you ever been burned?" Bill calmly replied, "Of course I've been burned. But I continue to have the opening bid of trust. Jim, it comes down to this. It's upside and downside. I choose to believe there's a much greater upside in trusting people and a much greater downside in not trusting people."

"For Bill," Jim explained to me, "it was the great flywheel effect in that the best people engage with the best people. And the most trusting people engage with the most trusting people. And Bill's view was, 'If you have an opening bid of trust, the best people will be attracted to that, and it will serve as a magnet. It will bring those people to you, and it will also help them be more trustworthy. If you trust people, you're going to change their behavior to be more trustworthy. Your trust will make them want to be worthy of that trust if they're the best people. So you win on all dimensions. And think about the downsides of not being trusting. The best people are going to be repelled by someone who doesn't lead with trust.'"[4]

The wisdom of Bill Lazier, shared with me by Jim, resonated with my own experience. It reminded me of a moment in my career when I was in a mid-level leadership position, working for a new boss. As the transition from my old boss to the new boss was happening, I was working to fill an open position on my team. The top candidate I wanted to hire was someone whom I identified as having "minimal experience with a very high ceiling." While the candidate lacked experience normally expected for the position, he had proved to me that he was a deep thinker, highly intelligent, and had a remarkable work ethic. While it would take some extra coaching to make up for his lack of experiential knowledge, I was willing to accept the responsibility for doing that work because I saw a huge upside.

I made the decision to hire this candidate and worked with my human resources partner to extend a formal offer letter. The very next day, I received a phone call from my new boss. He was irate: "*What are you doing?* He doesn't have enough experience! You can't hire that guy!"

"Have you spoken with him?" I responded.

"No." My boss was uninterested. "I don't need to speak with him. He's too young and doesn't have enough experience."

"I think you might change your mind if you speak with him. How about I set up a call?" *Trust me*, I thought. *I'm sure you'll see what I see.*

"*No!* You are not hiring him! I don't need to talk to him."

"I am sorry," I countered, "but I have already given him my word and sent him a written offer."

"Then rescind it. Take it back. We aren't hiring him."

I could not believe what I was hearing. "I gave him my word; I'm not taking it back. You have to trust me." Wasn't this obvious?

I will never forget his response: "You haven't earned my trust. I don't trust you yet."

He would not be my boss for long. From the moment of that phone call, I knew my time working for him would come to an end as soon as possible. There was no way I was going to work for someone who not only didn't trust me but did so by default without me having done anything to show myself untrustworthy. I left that job as soon as I was contractually able to, despite my team meeting 100 percent of our goal. High performers, those who want to do excellent work, will be repelled by people who don't lead with trust. It's just that simple.

Trusting others has a momentum-building effect that attracts high-caliber people and results in an organization full of excellent individuals thriving in a culture of trust. With trust as a foundation, the flywheel is set in motion and starts spinning ever faster as others buy in. This leads to even greater trust, which attracts more excellence-seeking people. We all can make the trust wager in each of our relationships every day.

STAY AWAY FROM THE POISON

How do you process it when someone wrongs you? How do you respond when life hands you circumstances that are as unfair as they are hard?

How would you handle something like Ed Latimore's life growing up? Could you do with it what Ed has?

Before he became the professional boxer turned competitive chess player, college graduate, Army vet, bestselling author, and inspirational speaker that he is today, Ed was raised by a single mother in the housing projects of Pittsburgh, Pennsylvania. He describes his childhood as one in which he "fought a lot, suffered physical abuse, observed a lot of violence, and even saw someone get killed once."[5] These brutal experiences gave Ed every reason to be justifiably angry and bitter. As a child, he survived his situation by retreating to books and video games. As a young adult, alcohol became his go-to coping mechanism.

And yet, Ed has a remarkable perspective that shapes his views of society and how he behaves in it. He told me, "No one cares what happened to you or what you've been through. No one is coming to save you." Ed's worldview is one of maximum accountability influenced by his study of Stoicism. *"Society is not going to take pity on you if your problems create problems for others.* You need to work through your own issues and your actions. Don't take your trauma out on others. If I commit a crime and do something awful to someone else, the judge doesn't care about my upbringing or all the prior bad experiences in my life . . . he's sending me to jail for committing a crime."[6] If your problems create problems for others, you won't get very far in life.

How has Ed overcome his childhood to gain such perspective? What was the key he used to grow beyond his victimization, while not becoming a victim? "It's about delivering value to others, and not subtracting it. That's destructive. Forgiveness is a powerful idea. Holding a grudge is like drinking poison and expecting the other person to die."

Much like Donald Miller (whom you read about in the previous chapter), Ed made the conscious choice to switch his perspective. He went from viewing himself as a victim to behaving as the hero of his story. Instead of sulking about the unlucky situation he was born into, he decided to do something about it. He worked his butt off in the classroom so he could go to college. He trained in the gym to become a professional boxer. He enlisted in the military to serve his country and become more disciplined. He learned chess to expand his mind. He studied Stoicism and applied its lessons to calm himself. He also got help to rid his life of alcohol.

None of those actions were easy. None of them came naturally to Ed. He was raised in an environment where it was normal to abuse drugs and alcohol. He witnessed others breaking the law. Instead of letting himself become what he saw, he made a change, knowing that if his problems created problems for others, society would not take pity on him. This is a harsh reality, but true. We are not all born into fortunate circumstances. Instead of indulging in the toxic poison of holding onto his bitterness, Ed Latimore understands the hand he was dealt, and is playing it to the best of his ability. He chose the freedom that comes from acceptance, forgiveness, ownership, and responsibility. This is something we all can do.

NEVER STIFLE A GENEROUS IMPULSE

Ask Jim Collins to talk more about what it means to pursue excellence in working with others, and again the name of Bill Lazier rolls off his tongue. "One day, two large wooden crates appeared on our front porch," Jim began telling me, "the address labels indicating they'd been shipped by Bill. He sent us a few dozen bottles of spectacularly good wine. I called and asked him what prompted him to send them to us, and he said, 'Dorothy and I had an inventory problem in our wine cellar, and we needed to make room for some new bottles. We thought you could help us out by taking some of it off our hands.'"

Bill has mastered the art of getting people to accept his generosity, somehow framing it as if you were doing him a favor. Bill was not just unloading wine he didn't want because he no longer had room for it in his cellar. He had paid close attention during a dinner he had recently with Jim and Joanne (Jim's wife). During that dinner, the Collinses had commented about how much they enjoyed Bill's selection of wine. For Jim and Joanne at the time, wine of such quality was a luxury they could not have afforded to stock themselves. So Bill decided to share and used his "inventory problem" as the excuse to do so without making the Collinses feel uncomfortable in the process.

The gift left a mark on Jim long after the wine bottles had been emptied. His takeaway was straightforward: never stifle a generous impulse. "The American Dream is not just about doing well for yourself," Jim explained. "It is even more about the opportunity to do useful work and to freely give of yourself to others."

"But what about the potential burnout of giving so much of yourself to others?" I asked. Jim replied, "Bill's generosity did not deplete his energy. Rather, it had the opposite effect. Because he was so generous and gave so much to other people, it came right back to him, increasing his gratitude, which he turned right back around into giving, which further increased his energy. 'Round and 'round the generosity-energy flywheel turned, building ever greater momentum throughout his life."[7]

When I think about most of the people in my life who live well, one behavior stands out: they are givers. Their impulse is to help other people. The list of people in this category starts with my dad. Growing up, I would regularly hear him late at night on the phone with people who needed to talk. He would patiently listen to what they had to say, ask some questions, and then offer some thoughts and advice. After he would finish, I'd say, "Who was that, and what did they want?" Sometimes he'd share their name and say, "They are going through a tough time. I'm just trying to help them out."

Not too long ago, I had the good fortune of being in the audience at my dad's retirement party. His company packed an auditorium with a standing-room-only crowd of several hundred people to celebrate his career. The CEO spoke about my dad's legacy, as did countless other leaders from across the business.

Tom Ogburn, my dad's longtime friend and colleague (and an incredible leader in his own right), served as the event's emcee. He started the celebration by asking, "Who here in this room has been directly impacted and helped by Keith Hawk?" The *entire room* stood up.

My dad's motto when it comes to helping others is: "Don't say no if you can say yes." If a brand-new entry-level salesperson wanted to have lunch with my dad, he would say yes. It might not happen right away (because he had said yes to so many others), but it would most definitely happen. Watching my dad's example, the ethic of "when in doubt, just try to help others out" was a fundamental part of the fabric of my upbringing.

My dad is the most giving person I've ever met, and it's no secret where it comes from: he learned it from his father. Just as with Bill Lazier, generosity is a natural impulse for both my dad and my Grandpa Hawk. They get pure joy out of giving, helping others, and seeing other people thrive. They do it because it's the right thing to do, and they don't seek credit or fame or compensation for it. For them, excellence doesn't just mean their own self-improvement; it means seeing others get another step closer to reaching their full potential.

One easy way to be generous is to be the person who spreads positive gossip. In our home, we've made it a family value: "We do not gossip negatively about others. Let's try to spread only positive gossip. If you have something negative to say about someone, tell them directly." The relational generosity of keeping criticism private while broadcasting good news about others is a wonderful attribute on which to build one's reputation. Be known as someone who shares great news in public and promotes the work of people you admire on social media, in emails, and in recommendations to friends.

"We have a tendency to define ourselves in opposition to stuff," says Australian comedian and musician Tim Minchin. "Try to express your passion for things you love. Be demonstrative and generous in your praise of those you admire. Send thank you cards and give standing ovations. Be pro-stuff, not just anti-stuff."[8] Opposing things is necessary at times, but being *for* something is more attractive, more effective, and more fulfilling.

PRACTICE GENEROSITY, HUMILITY, AND VULNERABILITY

"The great paradox of life is self-sacrificial service," says Brent Beshore, the founder and CEO of Permanent Equity. "The more I give, with no expectation of reciprocity, the better life goes for others and me. It's counterintuitive and countercultural."

Beshore loves investing in what he calls "boring businesses"—those steady and reliable family-owned companies that make things like swimming pools, aircraft parts, and glass. Permanent Equity invests for the long haul and operates from a first principle that suggests a physician more than a private equity firm: "Do no harm." Brent and his team prefer to work with existing management teams instead of making sweeping changes to the businesses once they invest. It is a strategy built on a foundation of humble generosity that seems as obvious as it is uncommon: lend your funds, time, and expertise to a business with a focus on making it *and the people already working there* better. Permanent Equity's investors don't give in to the temptation to make their investments about themselves, accelerating their profitable returns and putting their fingerprints on a company by imposing changes. "Why don't more investment firms take this approach? It seems to be working well for you," I asked. Brent answered without a hint of defensiveness or insecurity: "People pay attention to outliers . . . not the get-rich-slow style that we like. The slow-growth person isn't on magazine covers."[9]

When I interviewed Brent, I was struck by his rare combination of intellect, kindness, and humor. He's one of the highest signal conversationalists I've ever met. His responses were simple yet well thought out, coming from knowing himself well and delivered with a calming presence. He told me, "The best leaders know how messy they are. They challenge themselves. They have a high level of self-awareness. They know they need people around them to help. They acknowledge their imperfections, and they give others grace for their imperfections." Brent takes his work seriously but doesn't do the same for himself: his professional bio on the firm's website lists "competitive tennis and bad golf" as his occasional interests.[10] He often injects humor into the conversation through self-deprecation and is quick to point out his own past mistakes. "I was too goal focused, overconfident . . . I was often wrong, but rarely in doubt. I was scared," Brent admitted to me during his appearance on my show.

We tend to be more trusting with those who are willing to be vulnerable, share when they've messed up and how they've learned from their previous mistakes to get better. Working to be more credible is a worthy pursuit. Building competence, living with a virtuous character, and caring for others leads to meaningful relationships and a fulfilling life. From a leadership perspective, isn't that the type of person you want to follow? Isn't that the type of person you want to be?

SMILE

Credibility is defined as "the quality or power of inspiring belief."[11] To effectively work with others, you must have it. The ancient Greek philosopher Aristotle broke down personal credibility into three fundamental parts: "intelligence (or competence), a virtuous character (or trust), and goodwill (or caring)."[12] Those are big categories that take sustained effort through good decisions and work over time, for sure. But there are also micro moves you can make to boost your credibility in the eyes of others. You'd be surprised how valuable simply smiling is in this regard.

Ryan Caldbeck is the founder and former CEO of CircleUp, an investment platform powered by technology. I asked Ryan to share one of the best pieces of life advice he'd ever received, and his response was surprisingly simple. "My mom talking to me about how important it is to smile and how to smile," Ryan wrote back to me by email. "Smiling connects people, smiling brings people in, smiling builds bridges. Smiling invites a next step, which becomes growth. . . . All else being equal, you choose the kid for your team who smiles. All else being equal, you go up to the person at the bar who is smiling. All else being equal, you hire the candidate who is smiling. I hope to be able to pass this along to my kids, too."

The credibility that comes from simply being the person in the room who is smiling is not just a function of appearance. Smiles can be *heard* to the same effect. Years ago, my wife, Miranda, was living in Reno, Nevada. She had a phone interview for an inside sales position at LexisNexis in Dayton, Ohio, which consisted of a 60-minute conversation with Rex Caswell, the same vice president of sales who had hired me. After Miranda's interview, Rex offered her the job without ever having met her in person (this was before I met her).

Later, when I asked Rex why he had hired Miranda, he said, "I could feel her positive energy and attitude over the phone. I could feel her smile, and I wanted that positivity in my organization." It turned out Rex's instincts were correct: Miranda went on to become a high performer for the company, earning LexisNexis's coveted Circle of Excellence award before ultimately earning a promotion to a management role. Miranda is intentional about her positivity. She makes that conscious choice every morning, and it is contagious. Making the decision to have a positive outlook, believing that the day will go well, and then putting that attitude into practice by choosing to smile has a compounding effect. As Jon Gordon, author of the international bestseller *The Energy Bus*, once told me, "Positive energy is high-octane fuel, as opposed to the sludge created by negative energy. You need to drive your life with positive energy if you want to be successful."[13]

BE PUNCTUAL

How you spend your time is a matter of your own choices. Whether your time is well invested or wasted is on you. But when your actions dictate how others spend their time, it's important to be very mindful of it. Too often this gets overlooked—that what you do with other people's time impacts the connectors of trust and respect that make excellent group work possible. The simplest way to build trust and show respect for others' time is by being punctual.

Being where you are expected to be when you're expected to be there shows that you respect others. When you show up late, you are telling the other person, "My time is more important than yours." Offering a quick apology—"Hi, sorry I'm late. [insert excuse here]"—doesn't change this. Of course, this demonstration of disrespect is rarely ever done intentionally. Instead, time somehow just "got away from" us, or the generally foreseeable "unexpected" (traffic, train was late, meeting ran long, etc.) delays us. However, if you tend to be late, there is only one way to break that tendency. You must create a system that doesn't allow you to be late.

"The life of George Washington was characterized by a scrupulous regard for punctuality," write Brett and Katie McKay. "When he asked a man to bring by some horses he was interested in buying at five in the morning, and the man arrived fifteen minutes late, he was told by the stable groom that the general had been waiting there at five." Washington had gone on to the other business of his day, "and he wouldn't be able to examine the horses again until the following week." Washington "ate dinner each day at exactly 4 o'clock, and when he invited members of Congress to dine with him, and they arrived late, they were often surprised to find the president halfway done with his meal or even pushing back from the table. To his startled, tardy guest he would say, 'We are punctual here. My cook never asks whether the company has arrived, but *whether the hour has come.*' And when Washington's secretary arrived late to a meeting, and blamed his watch for his tardiness, Washington quietly replied, 'Then you must get another watch, or I another secretary.' . . . For Washington, being on time was a way of showing respect to others, and he expected to be treated with the same level of respect in return."[14]

We've all been in a conference room or on Zoom waiting for the leader of the meeting to arrive. The people who showed up on time as expected are rightly perturbed when the host finally shows up 10 minutes late and says, "Oh, I'm sorry. I'm back-to-back all day. OK, where were we with this agenda?" Let's say there are 20 people in that meeting: that one person who showed up late just wasted 200 minutes (20 people times 10 minutes). Whether you are meeting with a group or for a one-on-one with someone else, be on time.

This was drilled into me by my sports background. Our football coaches demanded that we be early for everything. I vividly remember my first morning workout as an eighth grader going into my freshman season. The varsity coaches asked that I work out with them for the grueling early morning June and July sessions. I was told that the workouts started at 5:00 a.m. So I showed up at 4:50 to be early and ready to go. When I was dropped off by my parents, I noticed that all my teammates were already running a lap around the school and had almost finished. I asked, "What's going on, I thought I was early?" An assistant coach said, "You're late, we start in the weight room at 5:00 a.m. We warm up, running outside for 20 minutes before the lift." I've been productively paranoid about punctuality ever since that moment.

I know that may seem like an extreme example, but the point remains: show respect for others by being on time. Here are some ways to do that:

- If you're in charge of your calendar, avoid scheduling meetings back-to-back with no minutes in between. Allow time between meetings to give you an opportunity to think and reflect and then take action—or just go to the bathroom or have a snack.
- If you have to drive to the appointment, assume it will take longer than you think. Assume there will be traffic. Don't use that as an excuse to be late. Give yourself a buffer.
- Start your meetings on time with no excuses. Every time. My dad always used the phrase, "We're going to honor the present," and then started his meetings on time every time. I try to do the same. Eventually, people who meet with you will learn that you are someone who honors the present and respects your own time and theirs by starting on time.
- If you called the meeting, end it on time. If that means you didn't get a chance to cover everything you had hoped to, then schedule another meeting or finish over email. Don't try to solve this problem of yours by stealing other people's time and putting them in a tough spot with their next obligation.

▶ If you didn't call the meeting, leave meetings on time. I realize this might be a challenge if you're in one of your boss's meetings. However, cover this with your boss in your one-on-ones. Explain that punctuality is important to you and you value showing respect for others by being on time. Maybe you can even help your boss get better at this (both starting and ending on time).

LISTEN WITH YOUR EYES

Early in my business career and after I had put together a couple of good years of overperformance as a sales professional, I and 14 other high performers were invited to a roundtable meeting with the CEO of our company (LexisNexis), Mike Walsh. Walking in, I felt the typical nerves of a young professional in his twenties who is about to have a face-to-face meeting with the CEO, someone I had only seen in person giving keynote addresses. Now, here I was, sitting at the same table, and he was asking us questions. They were what I now know to be the standard fare for these types of corporate leadership outreach meetings: "What do you like most about your job?" "What should we change?" "How could we be better?" "How can we make this an even better place to work?" At the time, however, they didn't feel standard to me. I was amazed that Mike was taking the time to meet with us and ask them at all.

As the conversation began to flow, I moved past being impressed and honored to be there and started paying attention to how he was conducting himself. Mike listened and asked questions. He took a few notes, but he wasn't writing excessively. I could tell it was important to him to look the person who was talking in the eyes and show that person respect. He listened intently, always asked a follow-up question, and was not afraid to sit briefly in silence to think. Mike did this with every person in the room. But it wasn't just a series of one-on-one conversations like in some formal receiving line at an event. While talking directly to the person who was fielding his question, he also created the sense of security and freedom in the room for someone else to speak up without being posed a direct question. It was an impressive display of leadership through communication.

But what was even more remarkable was how he ended the meeting. Mike summarized our entire meeting and discussed the high points to ensure we felt heard. In fact, he used the *exact words* that we had spoken and attributed them to each person who had said them. He made people feel heard and that he truly cared. As we all walked out of the room, the impression I had was not lost on anyone else in the group. "Wow, I knew he was smart, but I didn't realize he was that good!" said one person. "He actually listened to us! He cares what we think!" said another.

After I left the conference room, I continued to analyze the meeting and my observations. Later in the day, I realized a few keys to why he had felt so sincere, and in turn, why our engagement with Mike was so good.

- ▶ **He listened with his eyes.** He looked directly at the person speaking, gave knowing nods, and showed that he cared about what they were saying—all with his eyes.
- ▶ **He made it about us.** He was the CEO of a multibillion-dollar global corporation. Nobody would have been surprised if he had used the time to deliver a 20-minute speech about our business in the same way some politicians use town hall meetings with their constituents: as a message-spreading event rather than a true listening exercise. Instead, he said, "This meeting is about you and me learning from you. I'll ask some questions, but please feel free to speak up at any moment to share how things are going." It wasn't about him. It was about us.
- ▶ **He made mental notes.** During the session, Mike occasionally wrote down a few notes. For the most part, he remembered what we said without referencing his notes. His focus was on engaging with us more than recording our answers or using note-taking as a pose for listening. By focusing on listening, he was able to distill our messages to their essence and share the critical points

back with us. It seems trivial, but it's really a big deal. We felt a tremendous amount of respect as low-level, frontline employees by his display of deep, focused attention on what we were saying. This is a rare skill, but it's obvious he had worked on it and gotten very good at it.

Think about the conversations you're having daily. What percent of the time are you talking? How many questions are you asking? Are you listening with your eyes? How many follow-up questions are you asking? The most excellent people I've encountered lead with curiosity: they ask more questions than they answer. They genuinely want to learn from the other person. They distill what they hear and reframe their responses based on that information. In the process, they show others respect. They build the kinds of relationships that are key to living a life of excellence.

CREATE YOUR JUNTO

In the fall of 1727, 21-year-old Benjamin Franklin and a group of friends founded the Junto.[15] The purpose of the 12-member club of tradesmen and artisans was mutual improvement. Members of the Junto were avid readers and intellectuals who met to discuss questions of the day and to exchange knowledge of business affairs.

In his autobiography, Franklin spelled out what being a member of the Junto required and delivered:

> We met on Friday evenings. The rules that I drew up required that every member, in his turn, should produce one or more queries on any point of Morals, Politics, or Natural Philosophy, to be discussed by the company; and once in three months produce and read an essay of his own writing, on any subject he pleased.
>
> Our debates were to be under the direction of a president, and to be conducted in the sincere spirit of inquiry after truth,

without fondness for dispute or desire of victory; and to prevent warmth, all expressions of positiveness in opinions, or direct contradiction, were after some time made contraband, and prohibited under small pecuniary penalties.[16]

This practice of seeking to improve yourself and your environment by regularly meeting with peers of like minds (seeking to learn and grow) but of varied interests (what they already know and have experienced) has a long history. During my conversation with bestselling author and Stoicism student Ryan Holiday, he told me about the Scipionic Club in ancient Rome.[17] Three men—a stoic philosopher named Panaetius, a fellow student of Diogenes named Gaius Laelius, and Scipio Aemilianus, one of Rome's great generals—created a philosophical club known to historians today as the Scipionic Club. The trio would meet to discuss and debate the stoic philosophy to which they all subscribed. First-century Greek scholar Plutarch wrote about this gathering in his *Moralia*: "it is a fine thing also, when we gain advantage from the friendship of great men, to turn welfare of our community, as Polybius and Panaetius, thru Scipio's goodwill towards them, conferred great benefits upon their native states."[18]

For the last several years, I have had the good fortune of experiencing the benefits of meeting regularly with my own Junto through my Learning Leader Circles. The intention behind the Circles was simple: to create Junto-like communities of growth-oriented individuals with intention and deliberation. The first group that I formed in 2017 remains active. I have since created additional circles. Leading my circles is some of the most rewarding work that I do. I send prework to the group, we do the work, and then we meet to discuss it via Zoom. We have members from all over the world. Here are some of the keys to getting a successful Junto up and running:

▶ **Get the people right.** I created an application process, and I personally interview all the candidates who make it past the written application. It's *all* about the people. I am fanatical about ensuring that members have a give first mentality. The first questions I ask each applicant are, "How will you make this group better? What unique quality will you bring to the group?"

▶ **Structure the meetings ... but not too much.** There is written prework for each meeting, but I've learned that some of the most impactful sessions develop after we have gone off topic. Maybe someone is dealing with a tragedy or a challenge at work, and they need advice. Having 12 other thoughtful, empathetic, generous peers to go to for encouragement and support has been an asset for the members.

▶ **Make the meetings different.** I intentionally meet with my groups for 75 minutes, every three weeks. Why? Very rarely do you meet for that length of time. Most meetings are the lengths of time defined by day planners and Outlook calendars: either one hour or half an hour. I want our members to notice a difference on their calendars when they see the meeting invite. "Seventy-five minutes? That doesn't look right? Ah, that's my Learning Leader Circle meeting." This also is a length that is long enough to go deep, but not long enough to get boring.

▶ **Lead with vulnerability.** I share more with my Learning Leader Circle members than any other group of people (outside of my immediate family). They know more about me than anyone else. When the leader goes first, it opens the door for others to do the same. It is not abnormal for tears to be shed during our meetings. The bond formed among the group strengthens quickly when people lower their guard and share their true vulnerabilities. I request that all members turn their cameras on when meeting through Zoom. Seeing each other's faces is important.

▶ **Get together in person at least once a year.** The relationship with our group grew to another level after our first in-person get-together. My first group all flew to Dayton, Ohio, and spent three days together. We had dinner at my home and answered personal questions to get to know each other more deeply. We had a small workshop session together. We did improv training together. We listened to a few remarkable keynote speakers together. Those three days were a critical inflection point for our group. The experience incubated our relational connections with each other.

▶ **Follow up.** Take notes during the meetings. Write down all the key resources mentioned, and then send a follow-up email recapping the meeting. This is something I started doing as a manager early in my career and have found that the recap emails have always been appreciated.

Think about how you can create your own Junto. While my Learning Leader Circles are part of my business offerings, this concept is useful for anyone interested in pursuing mutual improvement through the careful curation of a group of thoughtful people who want to help others. Build yourself a Junto like that, and I promise you won't regret it.

9

IT'S A LIFELONG PURSUIT

*Maybe that's enlightenment enough: to know that there
is no final resting place of the mind; no moment of smug
clarity. Perhaps wisdom . . . is realizing how small I
am, and unwise, and how far I have yet to go.*
—Anthony Bourdain

The greatest sushi chef in the world was born in Tenryu, Japan, on October 27, 1925. At the age of just seven years old, Jiro Ono began working in a restaurant. He became a qualified sushi chef in 1951 and opened his own restaurant in 1965. His restaurant, Sukiyabashi Jiro, has earned the Michelin Guide's top three-star status every year from 2007 to 2019,[1] despite being in a subway station in the basement of an office building in Tokyo and having a seating capacity of just 10 people. If you'd like to eat there, be prepared to make a reservation more than a month in advance. The cost? $375 for a *15-minute* dining experience. During an official diplomatic trip to Japan, President Barack Obama was invited by the Prime Minister of Japan to a meal at Sukiyabashi Jiro. "I was born in Hawaii and ate a lot of sushi," the president said after the meal, "but this was the best sushi I've ever had in my life."[2]

The culinary mastery of Jiro was the subject of a documentary, *Jiro Dreams of Sushi* (because Jiro would dream of sushi at night and jump out of his bed with new ideas). So how does a 95-year-old remain the best in the world at his profession? When asked about his philosophy toward work, Jiro said, "Once you decide on your occupation, you must immerse yourself in your work. You have to fall in love with your work. Never complain about your job. You must dedicate your life to mastering your skill. That is the secret to success." He added, "All I want to do is to make better sushi. I do the same thing over and over, improving it bit by bit. There is always a yearning to achieve more. I'll continue to climb, trying to reach the top, but no one knows where the top is. I've never once hated this job and gave my life to it. . . . Even at my age, after decades of work, I don't think I have achieved perfection."[3]

Excellence is about the lifelong pursuit of improvement. It is the drive for perfection (which can never be attained) that leads to the development of mastery. In the process, your achievements will benefit others and the world, but the real payoff for someone like Jiro is the internal satisfaction that comes from professional mastery. Take a deeper dive to understand how Jiro sustains excellence to better understand how we can do it ourselves:

- ▶ **Mistakes.** When a mistake is made at his restaurant, someone will point out what could be done better, it is acknowledged, and it is immediately corrected. When something below the standard is recognized, the response is a quick *hai*, meaning, "yes, I understand."
- ▶ **Preparation.** "If you apply for a job at Jiro's sushi bar," says Blossom CEO Thomas Schranz, "you know what you are getting yourself into. It will take about 10 years of dedicated work until you'll be allowed to cook *tamagoyaki* (egg sushi). It takes a long time of training and personal growth until Jiro considers you a *shokunin* (master craftsman)."[4]
- ▶ ***Shokunin.*** "The Japanese word shokunin is defined by both Japanese and Japanese-English dictionaries as 'craftsman' or 'artisan,' but such a literal description does not fully express the deeper meaning," explains artist Tasio Orate. "The

Japanese apprentice is taught that shokunin means not only having technical skills, but also implies an attitude and social consciousness. . . . The shokunin has a social obligation to work his/her best for the general welfare of the people. This obligation is both spiritual and material, in that no matter what it is, the shokunin's responsibility is to fulfill the requirement."[5]

▶ **Improvement.** Initially, Jiro would massage the octopus 30 minutes prior to preparing and serving it to his guests. Because of his mindset to always improve, he experimented with massaging it 40 to 50 minutes, finding that it ensures an extra tender texture. Did people love it when he worked on it for 30 minutes? Absolutely. And yet, he found a way to make something that was already excellent better.

How can you embody the ethos of Jiro to pursue and sustain excellence? It requires a mindset of a lifetime commitment to continually improve your skills and strive to make your work better. As Jiro says, "I'll continue to climb trying to reach the top, but no one knows where the top is."[6]

THE GOOD FORTUNE OF KNOWING NOTHING

Half a century ago, a Zen monk named Shunryu Suzuki published his seminal work of Zen Buddhism, *Zen Mind, Beginner's Mind*. In his book, the founder of the first Zen monastery outside of Asia discusses the concept of *shoshin*. It refers to having an attitude of openness, eagerness, and lack of preconceptions, even when studying at an advanced level, just as a beginner would. Suzuki outlines the framework behind shoshin, noting, "in the beginner's mind there are many possibilities, but in the expert's mind there are few."[7]

A few years ago, I purchased a print of the image in Figure 9.1 and hung it up in my office.

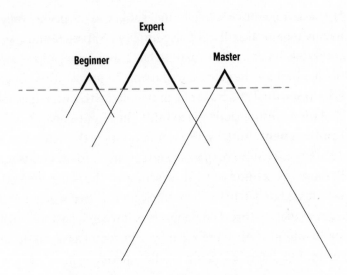

FIGURE 9.1　**True mastery kills the ego**

Source: Joey Roth. Used with permission.

As a beginner, we tend not to have much to say because we don't know much. Our minds are open, and we have a hunger to learn. We are willing to learn and consider all pieces of knowledge and information. Beginners have the curiosity of a child and a lack of fear of asking "dumb" questions because their desire to learn outweighs their fear of looking stupid. This is the "rookie" that Liz Wiseman talks about in her book, *Rookie Smarts: Why Learning Beats Knowing in the New Game of Work.*

With time, education, and experience, the deep understanding of expertise comes, but not without its own risks. There is danger in becoming an expert who already knows everything and doesn't want or need new information. Experts have arrived. They live to talk about their expertise and see their ideas validated and confirmed. We've all experienced a few experts like this; you may have had one as a boss. They knew everything they needed to know. As a result, they didn't consider new ideas, didn't read books, and certainly didn't empower a team to contradict their expert opinion. What they confuse as learning is simply information consumption aimed in one direction—finding examples to prove their theories right and waiting until they hear something that aligns with their current philosophy or previous experience. You won't have to ask who is an expert; they won't miss an opportunity to tell you.

The mindset of mastery is different. In the paradigm of shoshin, a master speaks with the same volume as a beginner, but from a depth of knowledge that surpasses that of even the loudest experts. As we pursue mastery, life humbles us. In turn, we think more deeply and realize that we have so much more to learn. The minds of beginners and masters alike are open and willing to entertain different ideas and to consider various perspectives. In his book *Fooled by Randomness*, Nassim Taleb captures the mindset of the master well: "My lesson from Soros is to start every meeting at my boutique by convincing everyone that we are a bunch of idiots who know nothing and are mistake-prone, but happen to be endowed with the rare privilege of knowing it."[8] The good news is that if you're reading this book, you are probably the type who enjoys having the good fortune of knowing you're an idiot. And that awareness is critical on your lifelong path to excellence and mastery.

PERSONAL MASTERY

People with a high level of personal mastery live in a continual learning mode. They never fully "arrive." Sometimes the term "personal mastery" can create a misleading sense of finiteness. But personal mastery is *something you do, not something you possess*. It's a verb, not a noun. It is an evolving process, a lifelong discipline. It flows with the never-arrived-always-becoming mindset that JJ Redick described when he and I spoke during his appearance on *The Learning Leader Show*.[9] People who strive for personal mastery have an always-evolving mindset born of a willingness to change their minds. They typically don't enjoy being part of an organization heavy into the that's-how-we've-always-done-it approach. People with a high level of personal mastery are acutely aware of their ignorance, their "conscious incompetence," and their growth areas. They are also deeply self-confident. This may sound paradoxical, but it is only so for those who do not see that "the journey is the reward."[10]

WHAT'S UNDER YOUR PILLOW?

As a child, Theodore Roosevelt was undersized and often sick due to his severe asthma. His parents weren't certain he would survive. Roosevelt would later admit that he was "nervous and timid." Young Teddy admired and looked up to men who were fearless. He spoke of having a great desire to be like those who could "hold their own in the world." When he was 12, his dad told him, "You have the mind, but you have not the body, and without the help of the body, the mind cannot go as far as it should. You must make the body." So Roosevelt decided to do something about it.

He created a process to build a strong body to go along with his sharp mind. He lifted weights, rowed, and boxed. By the time he graduated from Harvard, he had transformed himself into one of those men who could "hold their own in the world." This work ethic and devotion to the process of improvement would guide him for the rest of his life. After making a name for himself as a war hero for his action in Cuba during the Spanish-American War, Roosevelt served a term as governor of his home state of New York. Rather than run for a second term in 1900, the Republican Party tapped him to join the reelection ticket of President William McKinley as his vice president. Six months after McKinley was sworn in for his second term in office, his assassination suddenly made Theodore Roosevelt the twenty-sixth president of the United States at just 42 years old. He remains the youngest president in US history. Roosevelt steered the United States more actively into world politics, guided by his oft-quoted favorite proverb, "Speak softly and carry a big stick." He won the Nobel Peace Prize for mediating the

Russo-Japanese War, reached a gentleman's agreement on immigration with Japan, and sent the Great White Fleet on a goodwill tour of the world. At home, Roosevelt the Progressive built a presidential legacy by waging war on corporate monopolies and railroad tycoons; using government power to ensure that all sides in the economy got a "Square Deal"; and creating the National Park system to preserve America's wilderness and wildlife heritage.[11] He was an accomplished individual beyond anyone's measure of success.

On January 6, 1919, Theodore "Teddy" Roosevelt died in his sleep, prompting then Vice President Thomas Marshall to say, "Death had to take him sleeping, for if Roosevelt had been awake, there would have been a fight." The most interesting part? When they removed him from his bed, they found a book under his pillow. Even after a lifetime of accomplishment, he had continued to learn and improve himself until his very last day.

One of the most inspiring aspects of my work interviewing guests for my podcast is that I get an inside look at the daily practices of wildly effective leaders. Virtually all of them have the mindset of being a constant work in progress. They believe they have more to learn and never feel like they have it all figured out. Like Teddy Roosevelt, they are Learning Leaders. What process have you purposefully put in place to ensure you're learning something new each day?

THE FEYNMAN TECHNIQUE

A great way to ensure that you understand what you've learned about a new topic is to follow the process of the late, great Richard Feynman. Known primarily for his work as a theoretical physicist, Feynman was also an accomplished philosopher, teacher, and author. Among the many of Feynman's professional highlights, his groundbreaking research pioneered an entire field of scientific study: quantum electrodynamics (QED). Feynman's innovative way of visually explaining how various subatomic particles interact at a quantum level through

diagrams (now known as Feynman diagrams) helped scientists understand the interaction of light and matter and earned him a share of
a Nobel Prize in 1965.[12] In 1986, he utilized his gifts for visualizing a
concept and explaining it in simple, easy-to-understand ways as part
of the Rogers Commission Report into the disastrous explosion of the
space shuttle *Challenger*. Inspired by Feynman's work and his unique
way of teaching others, Bill Gates called him, "the best teacher I never
had."[13] As proof of the point, Gates secured the rights to publish the
videos of seven of Feynman's most famous lectures on scientific topics, the "Messenger Lecture Series," and made them freely available on
the web.[14]

But Richard Feynman's life and work can teach us more than just
about physics. Several writers have distilled from Feynman a process
for learning they have dubbed the Feynman Technique. This four-step
process is how Feynman himself tackled learning something new:[15]

1. **Choose what you want to learn about.** Take notes on
   everything you currently know about the topic. When you find
   new information, add it to your list.
2. **Teach it to a child.** Think about how you would explain
   something to a child. Children don't understand complicated
   jargon or acronyms. We all can picture that person in a
   conference room using big fancy words to sound smart. Do the
   opposite of that. If you can't teach it to a child, you don't know it
   well enough.
3. **Identify your gaps.** Ask yourself, "What am I missing?" Get back
   to the source material and formulate your thoughts based on
   what you currently know and the additional information you're
   downloading to your brain.
4. **Organize, simplify, and tell a story.** Gather your notes and
   create a simple, concise, memorable story. When I'm delivering
   a keynote speech, my framework is: Story + Science + Practical
   Application. I do this with a specific purpose. The story grabs
   the audience's attention and makes it memorable. The science

proves what I'm saying is true. The practical application piece answers the questions ,"So what? Why should I care?" Think about the most impactful leaders you know, whether a boss, a coach, or a teacher. They are memorable because of their ability to weave fascinating stories throughout their message. They are informative *and* entertaining. Novelist Richard Powers said, "The best arguments in the world won't change a single person's mind. The only thing that can do that is a good story."[16]

This was what Feynman figured out. Use his technique to hone your ability to learn and tell a story. Practice telling these stories with those close to you. One of the actions that my wife and I regularly practice is summarizing a recent podcast episode or a book for the other. This forces us to understand the key learnings from that podcast or book and share what we found to be most useful. Often, it's a story. And we try to tell it in a way that engages, excites, and is helpful to the other.

When you're in information consumption mode (reading, listening to a podcast, meeting with a mentor), distill what you learned immediately, following the moment of consumption, in your notes. And then share it with someone else. When you do this day after day, not only will your knowledge compound, your *understanding* will deepen as well. Over time, you will find that you have become wiser, more informed, and in a better position to help share what you've learned with others in a compelling fashion. Like most things in life, consistent repetition is key.

STEP BACK TO MOVE FORWARD

When the 2012–2013 basketball season came to a close, the Runnin' Bulldogs of Gardner-Webb University had achieved something no other GWU team before had done: finish a season with more than 20 wins. With their final record of 21–13, the squad had posted the most wins ever in a season for the school since it graduated to Division I status 10 years before.[17] The success of Chris Holtmann's third full season as the team's head coach capped quite a turnaround for the program. In his first season, the team had posted 21 *losses*.[18]

But at that moment, Chris found himself at a crossroads. He had always had the ambition to be a head coach at the highest level of college basketball. In a short amount of time, he had turned the program around, and the future for Gardner-Webb looked bright. If Holtmann and his staff could keep the team on its upward trajectory of improvement, making the NCAA tournament the following March for the first time in school history was a realistic goal. But with GWU located in the tiny town of Boiling Springs, North Carolina (2016 est. population: 4,819),[19] Holtmann didn't see a path to his dream of a big-time head coaching job. Not even being named the Big South Conference's Coach of the Year, which Chris had just accomplished.[20]

Thus, the crossroads. It had taken Chris 12 years working as an assistant coach to earn him the head coaching job at Gardner-Webb.[21] Now, he was being offered the head assistant coach position at Butler University. The choice Chris faced had no easy answer: he could keep being the head man in charge where he was, or he could go back to being an assistant coach. This wasn't the first time Butler had tried to lure Chris to Indianapolis, Indiana. Butler had previously been led by one of the most successful basketball coaches in the world, Brad Stevens, who had just left the program to become head coach of the Boston Celtics. Years earlier, Stevens had tried to recruit Chris to join his staff at Butler. Now, the NBA's newest head coach was helping to pitch the opportunity to Chris once again.

This time, Stevens's sales pitch worked. Chris decided to take the unlikely step back from head coach of one Division I school to assistant coach at another Division I school. "As I debated," Chris told me, "I realized that I couldn't blame myself for craving stability—it was only human nature, after all. We are drawn by the soft voice of consistency, the allure of a warm blanket of security in our jobs and lives. And while many of us willingly and happily give in to living within the status quo, the reality is that the world around us rarely remains motionless. The sun rises and sets, the seasons pass, and the world keeps moving and changing. It is only as we grow older and look back at life that we realize all that we have missed, all that we could have accomplished, had we simply pushed ourselves to break free of our fears."[22]

Early into Chris's second season at Butler, the world once again refused to stay motionless. When the team's head coach had to take a sudden leave of absence for medical reasons, Chris was named the interim head coach.[23] "You will be evaluated daily," his athletic director told him bluntly. Chris recounted the experience to me: "It was hard to hear, but it was the reality. I told my staff, we are going to coach by our convictions and our values." The daily evaluation period didn't last long. After posting five straight wins to start, including a game against fifth-ranked University of North Carolina, Butler rewarded Chris with an eight-year contract worth millions of dollars per year.

Just three years later, Chris was at another crossroads. Ohio State University had parted ways with its hall-of-fame coach, Thad Matta. The school's athletic director, Gene Smith, aggressively pursued Chris to be the Buckeyes' next head coach. Chris and his family were settled and living a fantastic life at Butler. He said, "As I found myself deliberating once again, I began to think back to the work of Stanford psychologist Carol Dweck on motivation and failure. Dweck drew a distinction between performance orientation and learning orientation. Children that believe that their intelligence is fixed typically give up on problems quickly, whereas those that believe their intelligence is malleable, conversely, stick with problems longer. Adults are no different. Those who are performance oriented are dissuaded by failure—they favor stability. Whereas those who are learning oriented embrace opportunity and eschew the status quo."

Once again, Chris and his wife, Lori, elected to leave their comfortable life and take on the next challenge. He has proven everyone who has hired him to be right. After leading Butler to three straight NCAA tournament appearances, he followed that up with two straight trips with OSU, making Chris one of only seven coaches (along with Mike

Krzyzewski, Jay Wright, Mark Few, Bill Self, Roy Williams, and John Calipari) to coach his team to five straight first-round NCAA tournament victories. None of that would've happened had Chris been afraid to pursue growth in whatever shape it was offered to him.

THE DINNER TABLE

The pursuit of excellence is not a solo effort. The effectiveness of your attempts to chase excellence will be impacted by the health of the relationships you build along the way. One of the simplest but most profound methods of fostering healthy relationships is sharing a meal.

Researchers at Cornell University spent 15 months studying the group meal-sharing practices at the firehouses of a large metropolitan fire department. Their study included information gleaned from in-person visits to 13 different firehouses (out of more than 50 across the department) as well as questionnaires to the nearly 400 officers throughout the 2,100-person fire department. Notably, the researcher's work revealed "significant positive correlations between work-group performance . . . as well as cooking together." In short, the study authors state, "eating together was significantly associated with unit-level performance."[24]

Outside of the world of social science and the unique brotherhood of firehouse kitchens, an example of the power of *commensality*—"the practice of eating together"[25]—comes from one of the great franchises in NBA history. Entering the first round of the 2010 NBA playoffs, the San Antonio Spurs were just a few seasons removed from their run of winning three championships in five years (2003, 2005, 2007). But their exit from the previous year's playoffs had been embarrassing: a first-round loss in just five games to the Dallas Mavericks. Up three games to one in their opening round rematch against the Mavericks, the Spurs suffered a humiliating 22-point defeat in Game 5.

Typically, head coach Gregg Popovich would meet with his assistant coaches in his hotel room after the game to review the tape. But before the game had even ended, "Pop" decided on a different postgame plan. Instead, he summoned a Spurs official during the game and asked him to call The Capital Grille, an upscale steak restaurant. Pop's message: tell them the whole team is coming there to eat after the game. In the locker room afterward, the future Hall-of-Fame coach had a message for his defeated team: "Hey, we're together. Let's eat. That's basketball. . . . We'll get back to work tomorrow."[26] The team responded with a 10-point, series-clinching win in Game 6.

"Dinners help us have a better understanding of each individual person, which brings us closer to each other—and, on the court, understand each other better," former Spurs guard Danny Green told ESPN. Former San Antonio center Pau Gasol attested to the uniqueness of the culture Popovich and his team dinners produced: "I haven't been a part of that anywhere else. And players know the importance of it as well—and how important it is to Pop." When Popovich is asked why he puts so much emphasis on team meals, he has said the key is to take people out of their element, have them experience new things, and learn from it together. Says another former player: "I was friends with every single teammate I ever had in my [time] with the Spurs. That might sound far-fetched, but it's true. And those team meals were one of the biggest reasons why. To take the time to slow down and truly dine with someone in this day and age—I'm talking a two- or three-hour dinner—you naturally connect on a different level than just on the court or in the locker room. It seems like a pretty obvious way to build team chemistry, but the tricky part is getting everyone to buy in and actually want to go. You combine amazing restaurants with an interesting group of teammates from a bunch of different countries and the result is some of the best memories I have from my career."[27]

In my own career, I have had a similar experience. Group dinners have proved to be critical in the development of my teams. Sharing a meal helps people get beyond their standard work personalities. I've attended a few workshops hosted by my friend Jayson Gaignard, host of Mastermind Talks and author of the book *Mastermind Dinners: Build Lifelong Relationships by Connecting Experts, Influencers, and Linchpins.* I have consciously modeled what I do at my dinner events after what Jayson does with his. When I conduct workshops or in-person meetups of my leadership circles, I make group dinners part of the package. As the host of the dinners, I often ask questions of each guest. I prepare small cards and carry them with me. Between dinner and dessert, I walk from person to person and hand each one a card. On them are personal questions that compel the participants to think deeply about themselves before sharing their answers with the whole group. As Jayson told me at one of his events, "Relationships move at the speed of vulnerability." It's not always comfortable, but when I conduct after-action surveys of my events, the card questions always pop up as a highlight for attendees.

I encourage you to do the same when hosting a group for a meal. The questions are the catalyst for in-depth conversation, and they bring people closer together. In turn, relationships strengthened like this will be a vital asset of support for you as you pursue excellence.

EXCELLENCE TAKES TIME

"Great things take a long time and bad things happen quickly. Rome wasn't built in a day and Hiroshima was wiped out in seconds," Ed Latimore told me.[28] He's right: if you want to produce excellent work, be prepared to put in the reps consistently for years.

Morgan Housel is the bestselling author of *The Psychology of Money: Timeless Lessons on Wealth, Greed, and Happiness.* During our conversation for his appearance on *The Learning Leader Show,* Morgan described why we get this basic principle wrong so often in our decision-making. "Progress happens too slowly to notice; setbacks happen too fast to ignore. There are lots of overnight tragedies but no overnight miracles. Growth is driven by compounding, which always takes time. Destruction is driven by single points of failure, which can happen in seconds, and loss of confidence, which can happen in an instant."[29]

It is the combined effect of each moment's micro actions that generate the results of your lifetime. It's not necessarily all the monumental life choices. While those are important, it is important to be cognizant of the magnitude of each small choice you make and the impact those have as your actions compound. The advice you often hear about long-distance running is no less true for being banal: no matter how far you have to run, you can only get there one step at a time. The same is true in the pursuit of excellence, whether in your business, in your relationships, or in your life generally. *Excellence is slow. Destruction is fast.*

In his book, *The Compound Effect*, author Darren Hardy emphasizes the power of small adjustments over time. Consider a plane traveling to New York City from Los Angeles: "If the nose of the plane is pointed only 1 percent off course—almost an invisible adjustment when the plane's sitting on the tarmac in Los Angeles—it will ultimately end up about 150 miles off course, arriving in either upstate Albany or in Dover, Delaware. Such is the case for your habits. A single poor habit, which doesn't look like much in the moment, can ultimately lead you miles off course from the direction of your goals and the life you desire."[30]

Maximizing the change-making potential of this phenomenon for the better requires thoughtful intention and consistent effort. Here are some examples of actions you can take to start the work of building excellence in your life:

▶ Choosing to wake up an hour earlier to move your body (stretching, exercise, hydration). That consistent choice will make you healthier and more productive.

▶ Choosing to eliminate the constant interruptions of notifications on your phone. That one small choice will impact your ability to focus over the long term.

▶ Choosing to remove food that contains sugar from your home. If it's not there, you can't eat it. Making that one small choice will have lasting outcomes on your health.

▶ Choosing to go on weekly dates with your spouse. That one decision will have lasting impacts on your relationship.

▶ Choosing to write down each day what you're grateful for transforms your mind to one of gratitude for what you have. That will have a lasting impact on your attitude.

Focus on the micro actions that you can control day in and day out. After a while, you'll look back and see the benefits of consistently building and watching the magic of compounding take shape.

CONCLUSION

On April 23, 1910, in Paris, President Theodore Roosevelt gave what would become one of the most quoted speeches of all time. Originally titled "Citizen in a Republic," the speech would later be known as "The Man in the Arena." "It is not the critic who counts," said Roosevelt, "not the man who points out how the strong man stumbles, or where the doer of deeds could have done them better. The credit belongs to the man who is actually in the arena, whose face is marred by dust and sweat and blood; who strives valiantly; who errs, who comes short again and again, because there is no effort without error and shortcoming; but who does actually strive to do the deeds; who knows great enthusiasms, the great devotions; who spends himself in a worthy cause; who at the best knows in the end the triumph of high achievement, and who at the worst, if he fails, at least fails while daring greatly, so that his place shall never be with those cold and timid souls who neither know victory nor defeat."[1]

Last night, Miranda and I took our dog for a walk. We've tried to make this a nightly habit to ensure the one-one-one time with each other that we love (but is not always easy to get while raising children). She said, "Knowing what you know now, isn't it crazy that you left your job to work on your podcast and start a leadership development practice when you did? I mean, you had no guarantee of any revenue or that it could even be a business, just a belief that you could do it." It was more than just my own belief. I'm grateful to have supporters and people who believe in me, first and foremost being Miranda. It would be tough to bet on myself without having her in my corner, backing me up.

Not everyone will understand your choice to bet on yourself and pursue excellence. About a month after I left my job as VP of sales at a large company, a friend and I took our children to a park. As we were standing side-by-side, watching our kids playing, he said to me, "Why would you do that? You had a job that a lot of people work decades to get. And you just left? I can't imagine doing that. Aren't you nervous about taking care of your family?" At the time, I was taken aback by the comment. Instinctively I replied, "I'm in a fortunate position with a very supportive wife who believes in me. And I want to bet on myself. I plan to make it work. I don't fully know how yet, but I've learned the value of consistently showing up every day with the intent to help others as my guide to going in the right direction."

Then I thought of Brené Brown, the research professor and best-selling author of several books, including *Daring Greatly* and *Dare to Lead*. She's written extensively about how to (or not) explain yourself to those who question you. She writes, "If you are not in the arena getting your ass kicked on occasion, I am not interested in or open to your feedback. There are a million cheap seats in the world today filled with people who will never be brave with their own lives but will spend every ounce of energy they have hurling advice and judgment at those of us trying to dare greatly. Their only contributions are criticism, cynicism, and fearmongering. If you're criticizing from a place where you're not also putting yourself on the line, I'm not interested in your feedback."[2] I imagine she would agree with French film director Jean-Luc Godard, who said, "He who jumps into the void owes no explanation to those who stand and watch."

While it's vital to surround yourself with people who are willing and able to give you candid feedback, don't mistake all the noise and chatter from those in the cheap seats for insight from your chosen personal board of advisors. Growing up, my dad told me, "If you choose to do anything of significance, people will talk and write about you. Never get too high from the praise or too low from the criticism. Stay composed."

ACCOUNTABILITY IS REQUIRED

Betting on yourself means more than just accepting the risk of failure. It also means accepting the responsibility of your own personal growth. It's your responsibility to own your development.

In 2019, I hosted an event for the Centerville Sonny Unger Foundation alongside Clark Kellogg. Clark was an All-American basketball player at Ohio State. He joined the NBA as a first-round draft pick by the Indiana Pacers, signing an endorsement deal with Converse for his own signature shoe, the "Special K."

After his playing career came to a premature end because of chronic knee issues, Clark transitioned to the world of broadcasting, eventually landing a job with CBS Sports in 1997. He has since become one of the premier voices of college basketball. He famously played against (and lost to) President Barack Obama in a game of "POTUS" at the White House, which was shown on TV before the NCAA tournament in 2010.[3]

On stage the night of our event in Centerville, Clark encouraged the assembled audience to "take control of your own development. That's your property . . . how you grow, who you become. You have to be intentional about owning that."[4]

According to research done by C. Jeffrey Waddoups, professor of economics at the University of Nevada Las Vegas, there was a 28 percent decline in employer-paid training provided to employees during the years 2001–2009. This pattern was evident across occupation, education, age, job tenure, and demographic groups.[5] Because of this, it becomes even more important for you to take control of your own development. Don't assume that anyone is going to do this for you or that it will be perfectly mapped out by your employer. Even if your company is willing to pay for training, you may have to be the one who seeks out the development programs you need, so that your employer can simply pay the bill. According to research conducted by the management consulting firm Korn Ferry, when managers rated themselves on 67 managerial skills, "developing others" came in dead last. Simply put: don't leave your professional growth up to someone else to manage.

Here are a few ways to exercise the responsibility of taking control of your own development:

- **Be intentional about your *who*.** Surround yourself with mentors, supporters, and sponsors who have done what you want to do *and* are willing to offer you honest feedback on a consistent basis.

- **Write.** Nothing clarifies your belief system like getting the thoughts out of your head onto the page. Get a journal. Create a regular writing habit.
  - ▷ Take it one step further and build your home base (your own personal website) and publish what you've learned. "Learning in public" is one of the greatest networking tools in the world. You'll attract other deep thinkers and people who are growth oriented.
  - ▷ Personally, publishing my work has been one of the keys to meeting many incredible people, whether they are Navy SEALs, corporate CEOs, or professional head coaches. Many have become friends, confidants, and in some cases, clients.

- **Combine a range of skill sets.** Robert Greene shared with me that one of the keys to excellence is building knowledge and skills and combining them in a unique way. For example, if you work in finance, master the skill of public speaking. Combining the skill of understanding the financial metrics of a business with that of standing up in a room and delivering a compelling talk will set you apart and help you grow your career.[6]

- **Mentor others.** While writing is one of the greatest learning tools in the world, teaching is a close second. Being a teacher forces you to spend time in deep thought and study. That process—learning the material, delivering the message, and then receiving feedback on how helpful you were—will make you a more more attractive person and colleague. And you'll grow immensely in the process.

▶ **Understand the definition of success in your role.** While this seems obvious, it's not always the case. When looking to grow yourself and your career, don't overlook the best way to accomplish this: being excellent at your current job. Ensure that you have vivid clarity on what excellence looks like. And then design your days to ensure you're exceeding the goal.

▶ **Interview your heroes.** Ask the senior leaders at your company (and others) if you can interview them. Whether it's a podcast or a written article, show others in your place of work that you're curious to learn. Doing this earns you ample time with key decision makers in your business and an opportunity to build meaningful relationships. As you gain skills interviewing others, you'll learn how they've evolved to attain the roles they have.

It comes back to who you want to be and what you are doing to become that person. No one will map the path for you. No one will pave the road for you. And no one will benefit from making the journey more than you will. All these facts point in a single direction: take ownership of your own growth and development.

PUBLISH YOUR WORK

In 2008, when LeBron James won his first NBA Most Valuable Player award but had not yet won his first championship trophy, a lively conversation about how to judge basketball players and teams was occurring online. On a message board forum known as APBRmetrics, users discussed the emerging field of advanced statistical analysis and how it applied to basketball. The analytical revolution that had occurred on the diamonds of Major League Baseball (popularized by Michael Lewis's 2003 book, *Moneyball*) was sweeping the NBA.

One of the more prolific participants on the APBRmetrics forums was Eli Witus, who was sharing his posts under a pseudonym. When Eli decided to publicly claim ownership of his work, he started his own blog to publish his analysis. Unbeknown to Eli, his work had caught the attention of decision makers in the NBA itself, men like Sam Hinkie. At the time, Hinkie was a vice president with the Houston Rockets, putting his prior consulting experience (Bain & Company) and MBA (Stanford) to use to unlock statistical insights into basketball. Hinkie had long been telling people around him, "If you see something awesome, send it to me, I'd love to read it."[7]

By the end of the day after Eli had published his first blog post, a handful of people sent it to Hinkie. He was impressed, calling it "wild" and "super interesting." After Eli posted his next article, another handful of people forwarded it to Hinkie by noon. Says Hinkie, "I'm like, oh my gosh, this is massively good. And the primitives you would have to understand to do this kind of work, not to mention alone, are massive." By the time of Eli's third post, Hinkie was getting his own direct notification via his RSS feeder. Here is how Hinkie described his reaction to that third blog post to Patrick O'Shaughnessy on his podcast, *Invest Like the Best*: "I read it quickly, and I just printed it out and walked it down to Daryl Morey's office, and I said 'I'm about to hire this guy. I haven't met him yet, but I'm about to hire him, today.'" Morey, the team's general manager, looked over the printout of Eli's work and agreed. "I get it. Let me know how it goes." Says Hinkie, "We still put [Eli] through our interview process, but if you ranked candidates, he came in as the number one seed based on his prior work, and that work was massively influential about how we thought about him."

That was in 2008. The Rockets hired Eli, not only to gain access to his analytical skill but also because "we needed him to stop leaking this stuff out to the internet," says Hinkie. From publishing his work and sharing it with others, Eli Witus landed a dream job before he even knew the opportunity existed. "He didn't have to say, 'Oh, I learn fast.'

It was obvious he learned fast," says Hinkie. "He didn't have to say, 'Oh, I'm hyper-passionate about this.' It was obvious he was."[8]

Since then Eli Witus has become assistant general manager of the Houston Rockets, the "No. 2 man in basketball operations."[9] The bigger point is that Eli loved basketball. He could have spent those 250 hours on his jump shot or on his basketball broadcasting skills instead of on his analytical work and his blog posts—and if he had, he'd probably still be working his same job. Instead, he found an intersection of his passion with an area of his ability and talent, and he developed in that direction. He was objectively excellent, and he appears to be striving continually to get better at his craft while having his dream job.

GO TO CAMP

Dr. Laurie Santos is a cognitive scientist and professor of psychology at Yale University. She has been a featured TED speaker and was listed in *Popular Science* as one of their "Brilliant Ten" young scientists in 2007. In January 2018, her course titled "Psychology and the Good Life" became the most popular course in Yale's history, with approximately one-fourth of Yale's undergraduate students enrolled.

I asked Dr. Santos what research shows are the common behaviors that drive happiness. She answered with three things:

- **Being socially connected.** Happy people prioritize connecting with other people.
- **Being others oriented.** Happy people tend to focus on helping others.
- **Being grateful.** Happy people tend to look for the good in the world and in their lives. They have a mindful posture of gratitude.

For nearly eight decades and counting, researchers at Harvard University have been conducting the Study of Adult Development—

"a longitudinal study that has been following two groups of men over the last 80 years to identify the psychosocial predictors of healthy aging."[10] Known as the Grant and Glueck Study, the work has tracked the physical and emotional well-being of two groups of people: 268 Harvard graduates from the classes of 1939–1944 (the Grant Study), and 456 men from very different circumstances—those "who grew up in the inner-city neighborhoods of Boston" (the Glueck Study) from the year 1939 to 2014.

The conclusion? According to Robert Waldinger, the fourth director of the ongoing study, the factor that surpasses all the rest in terms of correlated importance to long and happy lives is love. "The clearest message that we get from this 75-year study is this: good relationships keep us happier and healthier. Period," he explained from the stage at TEDxBeaconStreet in 2015. "It's not just the number of friends you have, and it's not whether or not you're in a committed relationship. It's the quality of your close relationships that matters."[11]

Kevin Hern is a senior financial analyst at a large pharmaceutical company who is living out Waldinger's thesis. Kevin is very good at his job and he loves the work, but ask him about an annual event called Camp Hern and he lights up. "The first gathering started in 2006. I realized I wasn't seeing the important people in my life enough, so I asked 10 of my friends to stay with me for the weekend." This meant those 10 friends had to find random places to sleep in Kevin's house, which was also home to his wife, children, and mother-in-law. While the quarters were initially tight, the bond it formed was intoxicating. The attendees promised each other they would make it an annual event.

In 2020, Camp Hern celebrated its fourteenth anniversary in Scottsdale, Arizona. Now, the group is more than twice as large, made up of 20 to 25 guys. Each year, Kevin plans the weekend in a different location in the United States. The schedule is packed with guest speakers, sightseeing, baseball games, fly-fishing, and mountain climbing, among other activities. Camp Hern even has a mission statement: "Provide a diverse group of mid-career professionals and seasoned executives with an opportunity to connect and build relationships in a fun, informal atmosphere." Kevin's vision for Camp Hern? "Encourage each other personally and professionally as we strive to impact our families, companies, and communities."

Kevin told me his goal for Camp Hern was to "feast on the stories of others." I asked him what the group values most, and he responded with a picture of simplicity: "Sitting around a patio, wearing T-shirts and shorts. There is no one videoing the talks, no crowds. We get real stories, and people really open up." In the words of an attendee, the Camp Hern experience "forces me to stop and be reflective and vulnerable. I don't do that anywhere else." It's about connecting with people who have become lifelong friends and forming deep bonds with others.

My conversation with Kevin reminded me of my talk with Scott Galloway, a marketing professor at New York University's Stern School of Business and bestselling author of *The Four*. When I asked Scott why he thinks so many people follow his work, he said, "Most men have trouble talking openly about their feelings. We have trouble expressing our emotions. Men want to do it, but don't. That's what I do."[12] Camp Hern does this, too, and I can't help but wonder if we'd all be better off if we had a Camp Hern to go to every year.

BE A GRIOT

During his acceptance speech for the 2019 Mark Twain Prize for American Humor, comedian Dave Chappelle took a moment to honor his mother and the guidance she gave him growing up. "My mother used to tell me even before I ever thought of doing comedy, 'you should be a griot.' And she'd fill me with every story of black life. . . . She's educated in African American studies, and she would let me understand the context in which I was being raised." Chappelle explained: "A griot was a person in Africa who was charged with keeping the stories of the village. Everyone would tell a griot the stories, and they would remember them all, so they could tell them to future generations. As they got older, they'd tell the stories to someone younger. And they say in Africa, 'when a griot dies, it's like a library was burnt down.'"[13]

Storytelling is a fundamentally human tool not just for storing and sharing information. It is also how we establish new relationships and deepen the ones we have. Stories connect us, building the familiarity and trust that are the foundations of a great relationship. And as we've seen, great relationships are the linchpin of a life of excellence.

I remember growing up, being fascinated by the stories told by my Grandpa Dean Hawk. He loves to share our family's history and his pride in the Hawk name. He'd tell us grandkids, "You're going to grow up and people will ask for your autograph. When you sign it, be proud of your name." He even put together a book of stories about all the work done by members of the Hawk family throughout history. I remember reading it and swelling with pride. My Grandpa Hawk is very much a griot. (He is 84 years old and doing great.) He loves telling the stories of the past, so that future generations will know what it was like working on a farm, going to the bathroom in an outhouse, and why he finally went to college at the same time that his son (my dad) did.

As a leader of your family, your workplace, and your community, *you should be a griot.* Work on recording and telling the entertaining and informative stories of the rich history of your life. Write them down. Share them with others. This practice helps you gain clarity of thought and will build pride in yourself, your work, and your family.

LEAVE FRESH TRACKS

In the wintertime in Dayton, Ohio, we get our share of snowstorms. A few days after a big snow, you're likely to see footprints on running paths, sidewalks, and areas of normal foot traffic. This past Sunday, I went for my run-sprint-walk workout and noticed tons of snow on the field where I run sprints. It was frozen powder without a single footprint (Figure 10.1). I wondered if I would be able to sprint given that almost a foot of snow had been dumped on the field a few days prior.

FIGURE 10.1   **The snowy field**

As I walked around the path to get to the field, I stepped on the prints of many others. I got to the open field and took a step and sank. The ice and snow got in between my pants and my boots. My feet were cold and wet.

But there's something about the feeling of leaving your mark where others aren't willing to go. I like thinking of life as a way to leave fresh tracks, of being willing to go where others haven't and do what others won't because it's uncomfortable. As we continue our pursuit of excellence, I encourage you to look for opportunities to leave fresh tracks somewhere (Figure 10.2). Develop the habit of doing something because it's hard, uncommon, and uncomfortable. That is where growth happens. That is how we get closer to excellence.

Put yourself in situations that force you to dig deep and find something inside yourself to weather the pain and keep going. This habit will better prepare you for the inevitable challenges that you will face and increase your odds of overcoming them and getting better each step of the way. Leave fresh tracks and put your own unique dent in the world on your pursuit of excellence.

FIGURE 10.2   **Leave fresh tracks**

EPILOGUE

"This I Believe"

As part of the leadership development work that Brook Cupps and I teach to leadership teams, we ask each participant to do an exercise called "This I Believe." The assignment was first created by Brook in the leadership class he teaches at Centerville High School. Here are the directions:

1. Write an essay expressing what you believe (values, behaviors, actions). When presented, it should be two to four minutes in length. It must end with "This I believe."
2. Create a movie, including pictures and/or videos, as you narrate your voiceover, which is the text of your essay.

My video is viewable on YouTube (https://youtu.be/7ydhMxalUoU).

The pursuit of excellence is about being better tomorrow than I am today. To do that, I must give everything I have toward that goal. As Steve Prefontaine once said, "To give anything less than your best is to sacrifice the gift."

Improving myself is about change, and change brings pain, so I value *temporary discomfort.* To pursue excellence means not just accepting the challenges life brings—it means embracing them.

I believe in lifelong learning, and I love to *learn from others* whose lives I admire.

I work to hold myself to high standards, and build the world I want to live in. It's important to me never to think "that's not my job" or wait for things to change, but to move proactively to improve myself and strive to help others.

I consider it critical to take *ownership* of my thoughts, words, and actions, and take responsibility for the consequences.

I believe *preparation is the greatest medicine for fear*, and it's a way to show respect for others. Whether I'm conducting an interview, giving a keynote speech, or meeting with a mentee, I can never be too prepared.

I believe in *giving*, to use what I've been given and what I've worked to earn and share it with others.

I believe in *building meaningful long-term relationships* because love is what life is all about.

To build those relationships, I *lead with trust*. I choose to assume the best in people. I've found that when I lead with trust, the people around me will work to keep it. If I get burned, so be it.

I believe in *spreading positive gossip*. Instead of defining myself by what I'm opposed to, I want to be known as someone who is *for* things. I believe in being generous in my praise of others. I write thank you notes and compliment people behind their back.

All of these qualities and actions reflect my core values—and living my core values leads me toward excellence. My values are thoughtfulness, thankfulness, curiosity, and consistency.

- ▶ To be **thoughtful**, I try to pause to think, reflect, and analyze my behavior. I try to seek first to understand before trying to be understood.
- ▶ Being **thankful** means I am grateful for what I have and whatever comes to me, easy or not. Gratitude promotes optimism, and it's contagious.
- ▶ I am **curious** because I am interested in learning about people. Learning about their stories, ideas, and what makes them unique. I love asking questions, learning from others, and going to bed a bit wiser than when I woke up.

▶ I am **consistent**. It's not sexy, but it is effective. Showing up every day for myself, for others, and for my work is essential to pursuing excellence.

Pursuing excellence is the best way I know to honor the gift that is life. *This I believe.*

ACKNOWLEDGMENTS

I find the term *self-made* peculiar. In my experience, nobody is self-made. We are all built and crafted by our *who*. We rise and fall to the level of our peer group. The people we're surrounded by are who we become. This book would not be possible without an amazing number of people. I am so grateful. Here are some of them.

Casey Ebro: Your belief in me and my ideas has given me more confidence and belief in myself than you realize. From our first conversation about my first book to the Zoom we had discussing this one, you've always believed in my work. You told me, "Ryan, your excitement for this book makes me excited. I'd love to work with you again"—and then you offered me my second book deal. Your willingness and ability to provide detailed feedback has made this book *much* better than it was when I turned in the first draft. Thank you.

Jim Levine: It is a joy to work with someone who not only is excellent at their job but is kind, curious, and extremely supportive. Thank you for continuing to represent me as my book agent and for offering up so much wisdom to help.

Sam Kaufman and Bert Bean: I'm inspired by how much you care about the people you serve: waking up at 4:00 a.m. to handwrite thank you notes, flying cross-country for the funeral of a parent of an entry-level sales professional, and investing a ton of time and energy to develop others. Thank you for believing in me and offering the opportunity to partner with Insight Global. I'm pumped for the future with you!

The Insight Global Team: Leadership Academy, IGU, and all of the amazing people at Insight Global, thank you for welcoming me with open arms. You inspire me to seek out wisdom, help others, and strive for excellence.

Mary Beth Conlee: Thank you for always being there to edit and make my writing better. You are a delight to work with, and you always offer useful feedback.

My former bosses and mentors: Rex Caswell, Dustyn Kim, Bryan Miller, Lee Rivas, Scott Schlesner, Sean Hough, Paul Speca, Sean Fitzpatrick, Mike Walsh, Tom Ogburn, Tom Osif, and Jeff Weaver. Thank you for providing guidance and feedback and for giving me a push when needed.

Bob Gregg and Ron Ullery: I learned how to work hard, be overprepared, respond to adversity, and inspire a group of people from you. I am so grateful my parents chose to move to Centerville, putting me in a position to have both of you as my high school football coaches.

Terry Hoeppner: Thank you for offering me a scholarship and providing me the opportunity to compete against Ben Roethlisberger for two years at Miami University. I wouldn't trade that experience for anything. Thank you for having my back and being supportive when it was time for me to leave.

Lance Salyers: Thank you for being the first set of eyes on my first drafts. Your ability to edit the rough parts into quality paragraphs is a superpower.

Listeners of *The Learning Leader Show*: Your feedback is my fuel. It's the juice! Thank you for your continued support and willingness to share your personal stories about how my podcast has helped you. It means more than you realize.

Members of my Leadership Circles: Brook Cupps, Casey Rodriguez, Joe Neikirk, Parker Mays, Nick DiNardo, Matt Kaminski, Steph Wernick-Barker, Larry Seiler, Jeff Estill, Chris Schlehuber, Nicci Bosco, Keegan Linza, Amanda Wilson, Josh Nicholls, Amy Arnold, Jordan Ott, Billy Murray, Richard Matricaria, Liam Murray, Steve Funderburke, Rob Ehsan, and JJ Blaiklock. Thank you for your vulnerability, honesty, and friendship.

My family: Mom, Pistol, Berk, Beth, AJ, and Laura, I will forever be grateful for your unyielding support. Thank you for always having my back and believing in me.

Brooklyn, Ella, Addison, Payton, and Charlie: Your curiosity, kindness, and positive attitudes make me so proud. Seeing you smile is the ultimate joy for me. I love you very much.

Miranda: I love your work ethic, grit, toughness, beauty, and love. I am so grateful we get to do life together.

NOTES

INTRODUCTION

1. McCullough, David, *The Wright Brothers* (New York: Simon & Schuster, 2015), Kindle edition.
2. Id.
3. "The Flight Forebears," Smithsonian Education, 2013, http://www.smithsonianeducation.org/educators/lesson_plans/wright/flight_forebears.html.
4. Hardy, Darren, *The Compound Effect* (New York: Hatchette Book Group, 2020), Kindle edition.
5. Steward, Graeme, "I Run to See Who Has the Most Guts," Graemestewart.com, blog post, March 4, 2011, https://www.graemestewart.com/i-run-to-see-who-has-the-most-guts/.
6. Vocabulary.com, s.v. "pursuit," accessed March 21, 2021, https://www.vocabulary.com/dictionary/pursuit.
7. Maxwell, John, interview with Ryan Hawk, *The Learning Leader Show*, "Episode #351: John Maxwell—The Laws of Leadership (Follow Them & People Will Follow You)," podcast audio, February 9, 2020, https://learningleader.com/maxwellhawk351/.
8. Sinek, Simon, *The Infinite Game* (New York: Portfolio, 2019), 8.

CHAPTER1

1. Vernon, Steve, "Living to 100: An Action Plan," *CBS Moneywatch*, February 12, 2016, https://longevity.stanford.edu/living-to-100-an-action-plan/.
2. Zaraska, Marta, "Boosting Our Sense of Meaning in Life Is an Often Overlooked Longevity Ingredient," *Washington Post*, January 3, 2021, https://www.washingtonpost.com/health/boosting-our-sense-of-meaning-in-life-is-an-often-overlooked-longevity-ingredient/2020/12/31/84871d32-29d4-11eb-8fa2-06e7cbb145c0_story.html.
3. Galloway, Scott, "Galloway on Follow your PASSION," YouTube video, from a talk about his book, *The Algebra of Happiness*, posted by "Wave

Your Arms," December 28, 2020, https://www.youtube.com/watch?v=
2jIia7aXins.

4. Newport, Cal, interview with Ryan Hawk, *The Learning Leader Show*, "Episode #316: Cal Newport—How to Choose a Focused Life in a Noisy World," podcast audio, June 23, 2019, https://learningleader.com /newporthawk316/.

5. McInerney, Laura, "Carol Dweck Floats like a Butterfly but Her Intellect Stings like a Bee," *Schools Week*, June 25, 2015, https://schoolsweek.co.uk /carol-dweck/.

6. Id.

7. Dweck, Carol, interview with Ryan Hawk, *The Learning Leader Show*, "Episode #140: Carol Dweck—The Power of a Growth Mindset," podcast audio, July 10, 2016, https://learningleader.com/episode-140-carol -dweck/.

8. Dweck, Carol, *Mindset: The New Psychology of Success*, paperback ed. (New York: Ballantine Books, 2008), 7.

9. "Lehman Brothers Declares Bankruptcy," History.com, last updated September 14, 2020, https://www.history.com/this-day-in-history/lehman -brothers-collapses.

10. Serhant, Ryan, interview with Ryan Hawk, *The Learning Leader Show*, "Episode #407: Ryan Serhant—How to Have Big Magnetic Energy (Million Dollar Listing)," podcast audio, February 21, 2021, https://learningleader .com/ryanserhant407/.

11. "Ryan Serhant," Bravo TV, accessed March 21, 2021, https://www.bravotv .com/people/ryan-serhant.

12. Gamboa, Glenn, "Billy Joel Honored by Steinway," *Newsday*, updated December 12, 2011, https://www.newsday.com/entertainment/celebrities /billy-joel-honored-by-steinway-1.3385000.

13. Bahler, Tom, "Billy Joel Magic—Tom Bahler on 'The Longest Time,'" YouTube video, from an interview for Have a Sleepover Productions, posted by "Have a Sleepover Productions," November 30, 2020, https://www .youtube.com/watch?v=H9Y8eYNZnwk.

14. Joel, Billy, "Billy Talks About His Songwriting Process," BillyJoel.com, November 14, 2011, https://billyjoel.com/news/37747/.

15. Dubner, Stephen, *Freakonomics*, "How to Change Your Mind (Ep. 379)," podcast audio, May 29, 2019, https://freakonomics.com/podcast/change -your-mind/.

16. Ward, Marguerite, "Steve Jobs Taught Guy Kawasaki This Surprising Lesson About Intelligence," *CNBC Make It*, October 31, 2017, https://www .cnbc.com/2017/10/31/steve-jobs-taught-guy-kawasaki-this-surprising -lesson-about-intelligence.html.

17. Id.

18. Feld, Brad, interview with Ryan Hawk, *The Learning Leader Show*, "Episode #378: Brad Feld—How to Collect Amazing People, Question Your Biases, & Build Community," podcast audio, August 9, 2020, https://learningleader.com/feldhawk378/.

19. "About Our Firm," Permanent Equity, accessed March 21, 2021, https://www.permanentequity.com/about.

20. Beshore, Brent, personal twitter feed, February 1, 2021, https://twitter.com/BrentBeshore/status/1356217673835827200/photo/1.

21. Varol, Ozan, interview with Ryan Hawk, *The Learning Leader Show*, "Episode #367: Ozan Varol—How to Think like a Rocket Scientist," podcast audio, May 31, 2020, https://learningleader.com/varolhawk367/.

22. Zenger, Jack, and Joseph Folkman, "What Great Listeners Actually Do," *Harvard Business Review*, July 14, 2016, https://hbr.org/2016/07/what-great-listeners-actually-do.

CHAPTER 2

1. Keh, Andrew, "Eliud Kipchoge Breaks Two-Hour Marathon Barrier," *New York Times*, October 12, 2019, https://www.nytimes.com/2019/10/12/sports/eliud-kipchoge-marathon-record.html.

2. Hutchinson, Alex, interview with Ryan Hawk, *The Learning Leader Show*, "Episode #308: Alex Hutchinson—The Curiously Elastic Limits of Human Performance," podcast audio, April 26, 2019, https://learningleader.com/hutchinsonhawk308/.

3. Clark, Benya, "5 Quotes by Eliud Kipchoge to Inspire Your Running," *Runner's Life*, November 30, 2020, https://medium.com/runners-life/5-quotes-by-eliud-kipchoge-to-inspire-your-running-7073fef47881.

4. Reynolds, Tom, "London Marathon 2019: Eliud Kipchoge on Freedom, Simplicity & Power of the Mind," BBC.com, April 25, 2019, https://www.bbc.com/sport/athletics/48055305.

5. Pearson, Rick, "Happy Birthday, Eliud Kipchoge," *Runner's World*, May 11, 2019, https://www.runnersworld.com/uk/training/a29699713/happy-birthday-eliud-kipchoge/.

6. "5 Quotes by Eliud Kipchoge."

7. Baseball-Reference.com, s.v. "Mike Trout," accessed March 22, 2021, https://www.baseball-reference.com/players/t/troutmi01.shtml.

8. Gammons, Peter, "Gammons: What Next Season Might Look Like, and What Will Be Missing," TheAthletic.com, December 4, 2020, https://theathletic.com/2234677/2020/12/04/gammons-what-2021-mlb-season-look-like/.

9. Biography.com, s.v. "Michael Phelps," accessed March 22, 2021, https://www.biography.com/athlete/michael-phelps.

10. Kerr-Dineen, Luke, "16 Mind-Boggling Stats from Michael Phelps' Legendary Career," *USA Today*, August 12, 2016, https://ftw.usatoday.com/2016/08/michael-phelps-race-2016-rio-olympic-games-career-stats.

11. "Why Michael Phelps Came Out of Retirement in 2013," Olympics.nbcsports.com, April 17, 2020, https://olympics.nbcsports.com/2020/04/17/michael-phelps-retire-2012-olympics-swimming/.

12. Rodgers, Joe, "Michael Phelps Explains Why He's Returning to 200-Meter Butterfly," Sportingnews.com, May 16, 2015, https://www.sportingnews.com/us/other-sports/news/michael-phelps-200-meter-butterfly-2016-summer-olympics-swimming/12ahilk7obhmm1k4oom05ttwk6.

13. Zaccardi, Nick, "Chad le Clos Says Michael Phelps 'Can Keep Quiet Now' amid Butterfly Trash Talk," Olympics.nbcsports.com, August 8, 2015, https://olympics.nbcsports.com/2015/08/08/michael-phelps-chad-le-clos-trash-talk-butterfly-swimming-world-championships-laszlo-cseh-olympics/.

14. Chambers, John, interview with Ryan Hawk, *The Learning Leader Show*, "Episode #406: John Chambers—Former CEO of Cisco: How to Grow from $70 Million to $40 Billion," podcast audio, February 13, 2021, https://learningleader.com/johnchambers406/.

15. TED.com, s.v. "Derek Sivers," accessed March 22, 2021, https://www.ted.com/speakers/derek_sivers.

16. Sivers, Derek, interview with Ryan Hawk, *The Learning Leader Show*, "Episode #364: Derek Sivers—How to Redefine Yourself, Make Big Decisions, & Live Life on Your Terms," podcast audio, May 10, 2020, https://learningleader.com/sivershawk364/.

17. Sivers, Derek, "Keep Your Goals to Yourself," filmed July, 2010, TED video, 2:59, https://www.ted.com/talks/derek_sivers_keep_your_goals_to_yourself.

18. Sivers, Derek, "Presentations → Keep Your Goals to Yourself," personal blog post, July 2010, https://sive.rs/zipit2.

19. Jarvis, Chase, interview with Ryan Hawk, *The Learning Leader Show*, "Episode 103: Chase Jarvis—28 Ways to Be More Creative," podcast audio, March 3, 2016, https://learningleader.com/episode-103-chase-jarvis-28-ways-to-be-more-creative/.

20. McRaven, Adm. William, interview with Ryan Hawk, *The Learning Leader Show*, "Episode #363: Admiral Williams McRaven—The Bin Laden Raid, Saving Captain Phillips, & Leadership Lessons for Life," podcast audio, May 3, 2020, https://learningleader.com/mcravenhawk363/.

21. Martin, Steve, *Born Standing Up* (New York: Simon & Schuster, 2007), Kindle edition.

22. Kelly, Kevin, interview with Ryan Hawk, *The Learning Leader Show*, "Episode 132 Kevin Kelly: How to See the Future . . . ," podcast audio, June 12, 2016, https://learningleader.com/episode-132-kevin-kelly-how-to-see-the -future/.

23. Kelly, Kevin, "68 Bits of Unsolicited Advice," altaonline.com, September 29, 2020, https://www.altaonline.com/a8695/kevin-kelly-advice/.

24. McPhee, John, "Draft No. 4," *New Yorker*, April 29, 2013, https://www .newyorker.com/magazine/2013/04/29/draft-no-4.

CHAPTER 3

1. Taylor, Bill, "What Breaking the 4-Minute Mile Taught Us About the Limits of Conventional Thinking," *Harvard Business Review*, March 9, 2018, https://hbr.org/2018/03/what-breaking-the-4-minute-mile-taught-us -about-the-limits-of-conventional-thinking.

2. Woodward, Orrin, "The Bannister Effect—Breaking Through the Four Minute Mile," blog post, January 24, 2011, http://orrinwoodwardblog.com /2011/01/24/the-bannister-effect-breaking-through-the-four-minute -mile/.

3. Taylor, "Breaking the 4-Minute Mile."

4. Wind, Yoram, and Colin Crook, *The Power of Impossible Thinking: Transform the Business of Your Life and the Life of Your Business* (New Jersey: FT Press, 2006), 23; McCarthy, Rachel, personal twitter feed, October 21, 2020.

5. McGowan, Michael, "How Roger Bannister and Australian John Landy Raced to Break the Four-Minute Mile," *The Guardian*, March 5, 2018, https://www.theguardian.com/sport/2018/mar/05/how-roger-bannister -and-australian-john-landy-raced-to-break-the-four-minute-mile.

6. Worldathletics.org, s.v. "Men Outdoor," accessed March 22, 2021, https:// www.worldathletics.org/records/by-category/world-records.

7. *The Power of Impossible Thinking*, 22–23.

8. McCarthy, Rachel, personal twitter feed, October 21, 2020, https://twitter .com/rmccarthyjames/status/1318969146898612224?s=20 (accessed March 22, 2021).

9. Morin, Amy, "This Is Why Most New Year's Resolutions Fail," PsychologyToday.com, December 31, 2019, https://twitter.com /rmccarthyjames/status/1318969146898612224?s=20.

10. Clear, James, interview with Ryan Hawk, *The Learning Leader Show*, "Episode #279: James Clear—How Tiny Changes Can Equal Remarkable Results (Atomic Habits)," podcast audio, October 22, 2018, http://bit.ly /jamesclearryanhawk.

11. Hardy, Benjamin, interview with Ryan Hawk, *The Learning Leader Show*, "Episode 247: Benjamin Hardy—The Best Self Improvement Book of 2018," podcast audio, March 4, 2018, https://learningleader.com/episode -247-benjamin-hardy-best-self-improvement-book-2018/.

12. Varol, Ozan, interview with Ryan Hawk, *The Learning Leader Show*, "Episode #367: Ozan Varol—How to Think like a Rocket Scientist," podcast audio, May 31, 2020, https://learningleader.com/varolhawk367/.

13. Moore, Kaleigh, personal twitter feed, October 12, 2020, https://twitter .com/kaleighf/status/1315652029021380615?s=20.

14. De Botton, Alain, personal twitter feed, July 19, 2017, https://twitter.com /alaindebotton/status/887702081758474240?s=20.

15. Bezos, Jeff, "2017 Letter to Shareholders," aboutamazon.com, April 18, 2018, https://www.aboutamazon.com/news/company-news/2017-letter -to-shareholders.

16. Id.

17. "Vice Admiral James B. Stockdale," United States Naval Academy Stockdale Center for Ethical Leadership, accessed March 22, 2021, https://www .usna.edu/Ethics/bios/index.php.

18. Id.

19. Id.

20. Collins, Jim, *Good to Great: Why Some Companies Make the Leap . . . and Others Don't* (New York: Harper Collins, 2001), 85.

21. Id.

22. Levine, Alison, "About Alison," alisonlevine.com, accessed March 22, 2021, https://alisonlevine.com/about-alison/.

23. Levine, Alison, interview with Ryan Hawk, *The Learning Leader Show*, "Episode 098: Alison Levine—Climbing Everest & Impressing Arnold Schwarzenegger," podcast audio, February 14, 2016, https://learningleader .com/episode-098-alison-levine-climbing-everest-impressing-arnold -schwarzenegger/.

24. Levine, Alison, quote on alisonlevine.com, accessed March 22, 2021, https://alisonlevine.com/expeditions/.

25. Frei, Frances, "How to Build (and Rebuild) Trust," filmed April 2018, TED video, 14:57, https://www.ted.com/talks/frances_frei_how_to_build_and _rebuild_trust.

26. Frei, Frances, interview with Ryan Hawk, *The Learning Leader Show*, "Frances Frei—How to Empower Everyone Around You (UNLEASHED)," podcast audio, June 30, 2020, https://learningleader.com/freihawk/.

CHAPTER 4

1. Blake, John, "He Was MLK's Mentor, and His Meeting with Gandhi Changed History. But Howard Thurman Was Largely Unknown, Until Now," CNN.com, February 1, 2019, https://www.cnn.com/2019/02/01/us/howard-thurman-mlk-gandhi/index.html.

2. Sinek, Simon, "The Infinite Game," YouTube video, 25:48, from a *New York Times* Event, posted by "New York Times Events" on May 31, 2018, https://www.youtube.com/watch?v=tye525dkfi8.

3. Seinfeld, Jerry, "Howard Stern & Jerry Seinfeld on Willpower and Love," YouTube video, 2:20, from *The Howard Stern Show* on May 20, 2020, posted by "Bull Moose Group," May 24, 2020, https://www.youtube.com/watch?v=0gJVPCUUGSk.

4. Koppelman, Brian, *The Moment with Brian Koppelman*, "Shane McAnally—07/07/20," podcast audio, July 7, 2020, https://podcasts.apple.com/us/podcast/shane-mcanally-07-07-20/id814550071?i=1000483131796.

5. Henry, Todd, Interview with Ryan Hawk, *The Learning Leader Show*, "Episode #394: Todd Henry—The Hidden Forces That Drive Your Best Work (The Motivation Code)," podcast audio, November 29, 2020, https://learningleader.com/toddhenry394/.

6. Maxwell, John, interview with Ryan Hawk, *The Learning Leader Show*, "Episode #351: John Maxwell—The Laws of Leadership (Follow Them & People Will Follow You)," podcast audio, February 9, 2020, https://learningleader.com/maxwellhawk351/.

7. Maxwell, John, interview with Ryan Hawk, *The Learning Leader Show*, "Episode #361: John Maxwell—The Essential Changes Every Leader Must Embrace," podcast audio, April 19, 2020, https://learningleader.com/maxwellhawk361/.

8. Rubenstein, David, interview with Ryan Hawk, *The Learning Leader Show*, "Episode #401: David Rubenstein—Launching a Business, Living with Purpose, & Loving Your Life," podcast audio, January 10, 2021, https://learningleader.com/davidrubenstein401/.

9. Obama, Michelle, *Becoming* (New York: Crown, 2018), ix.

10. Redick, J.J., Interview with Ryan Hawk, *The Learning Leader Show*, "Episode 217: JJ Redick—'You've Never Arrived. You're Always Becoming,'"

podcast audio, August 6, 2017, https://learningleader.com/episode-217-jj
-redick-youve-never-arrived-youre-always-becoming/.

11. Raveling, George, interview with Ryan Hawk, *The Learning Leader Show*,
    "Episode #281: George Raveling—Eight Decades of Wisdom: From Dr.
    Martin Luther King to Michael Jordan," podcast audio, October 27, 2018,
    https://learningleader.com/episode-281-george-raveling-eight-decades-of
    -wisdom-from-dr-martin-luther-king-to-michael-jordan/.

12. Mitnick, Steve, "Thomas Edison Encourages a Young Henry Ford," *Fort-
    nightly* magazine, April 2017, https://www.fortnightly.com/fortnightly
    /2017/04/thomas-edison-encourages-young-henry-ford.

13. Cowen, Tyler, interview with Ryan Hawk, *The Learning Leader Show*,
    "Episode #283: Tyler Cowen—The Path to Prosperity in a Disordered
    World," podcast audio, November 11, 2018, https://learningleader.com
    /tylercowenryanhawk/.

14. Cowen, Tyler, "The High-Return Activity of Raising Others' Aspira-
    tions," blog post, October 21, 2018, https://marginalrevolution.com
    /marginalrevolution/2018/10/high-return-activity-raising-others
    -aspirations.html.

15. Epstein, David, "Some Personal News: I'm a Podcast Host!," blog post,
    January 26, 2021, https://davidepstein.com/some-personal-news-im
    -a-podcast-host-2/.

CHAPTER 5

1. Gardner, David Pierpont, "William Redington Hewlett," Hewlett.org,
   accessed March 23, 2021, https://hewlett.org/about-us/hewlett-family
   -and-history/william-redington-hewlett/.

2. Id.

3. Jobs, Steve, "Steve Jobs on Failure," YouTube video, 1:42, from interview
   with The Santa Clara Valley Historical Association in 1994, posted by
   "Silicon Valley Historical Association," October 31, 2011, https://www
   .youtube.com/watch?v=zkTf0LmDqKI.

4. Id.

5. Konnikova, Maria, interview with Ryan Hawk, *The Learning Leader Show*,
   "Episode #371: Maria Konnikova—How to Pay Attention, Master Yourself, & Win," podcast audio, June 21, 2020, https://learningleader.com
   /konnikovahawk371/.

6. *The Hendon Mob*, s.v. "Erik Seidel," accessed March 23, 2021, https://
   pokerdb.thehendonmob.com/player.php?a=r&n=212&sort=place&dir
   =asc.

7. Carter, Alexandra, interview with Ryan Hawk, *The Learning Leader Show*, "Episode #374: Alexandra Carter—How to Ask for More (10 Questions to Negotiate Anything)," podcast audio, July 8, 2020, https://learningleader .com/carterhawk374/.

8. Immelt, Jeff, *Hot Seat: What I Learned Leading a Great American Company* (New York: Simon & Schuster, 2021), Kindle edition.

9. Kruger, Justin, and David Dunning, "Unskilled and Unaware of It: How Difficulties in Recognizing One's Own Incompetence Lead to Inflated Self-Assessments," *Journal of Personality and Social Psychology* 77, no. 6 (1999): 1121–1134, https://www.avaresearch.com/files /UnskilledAndUnawareOfIt.pdf.

10. Galloway, Scott, interview with Ryan Hawk, *The Learning Leader Show*, "Episode #396: Scott Galloway—Making Predictions, Sharing Love, & Turning Crisis to Opportunity," podcast audio, December 13, 2020, https://learningleader.com/scottgalloway396/.

11. Zenger, Jack, and Joseph Folkman, "What Makes a 360-Degree Review Successful?," *Harvard Business Review*, December 23, 2020, https://hbr .org/2020/12/what-makes-a-360-degree-review-successful.

12. Williams, Scott, "Listening Effectively," *LeaderLetter* newsletter, accessed March 23, 2021, http://www.wright.edu/~scott.williams/LeaderLetter /listening.htm.

13. Wofford, Chris, "Are Most Managers Bad Listeners?," blog post, January 26, 2018, https://blog.ecornell.com/are-most-managers-bad-listeners/.

14. As of the time of this writing, the Cleveland professional baseball team still has the "Indians" as their nickname. The team has announced that they are changing it in the future.

15. Hennessey, Jay, interview with Ryan Hawk, *The Learning Leader Show*, "Episode #380: Jay Hennessey—How to Build a Learning Organization," podcast audio, August 23, 2020, https://learningleader.com /hennesseyhawk380/.

16. Id.

17. Smith, M.K., "Peter Senge and the Learning Organization," infed.org, 2001, https://infed.org/mobi/peter-senge-and-the-learning-organization/.

CHAPTER 6

1. Oppezzo, Marily, and Daniel L. Schwartz, "Give Your Ideas Some Legs: The Positive Effect of Walking on Creative Thinking," *Journal of Experimental Psychology: Learning, Memory, and Cognition* 40, no. 4 (2014): 1142–52, https://www.apa.org/pubs/journals/releases/xlm-a0036577.pdf.

2. Jabr, Ferris, "Why Walking Helps Us Think," *New Yorker*, September 3, 2014, https://www.newyorker.com/tech/annals-of-technology/walking-helps-us-think.

3. Friedlander, Ruthie, and Savannah Walsh, "37 Powerful Women on How to Be Confident," *Elle*, March 6, 2020, https://www.elle.com/culture/career-politics/news/a19684/powerful-women-on-how-to-be-confident/.

4. Crosley, Hillary, "Beyonce Says She 'Killed' Sasha Fierce," *MTV News*, February 26, 2010, http://www.mtv.com/news/1632774/beyonce-says-she-killed-sasha-fierce/.

5. Butcher, Jack, interview with Ryan Hawk, *The Learning Leader Show*, "Episode #379—Jack Butcher—How to Visualize Value," podcast audio, August 16, 2020, https://learningleader.com/butcherhawk379/.

6. Lee, Jesse, "Poetry, Music and Spoken Word," blog post of the White House, May 12, 2009, https://obamawhitehouse.archives.gov/blog/2009/05/12/poetry-music-and-spoken-word.

7. Miranda, Lin-Manuel, "Lin-Manual Miranda Performs at the White House Poetry Jam: (8 of 8)," YouTube video, 4:26, recorded at the White House Evening of Poetry, Music, and the Spoken Word on May 12, 2009, posted by "The Obama White House," November 2, 2009, https://www.youtube.com/watch?v=WNFf7nMIGnE&list=LLgpWNZH1NDeqxZC5auw3Hxw&index=2996.

8. Miranda, Lin-Manual, "Lin-Manual Miranda Recalls His Nerve-Wracking Hamilton Performance for the Obamas," YouTube video, 3:44, interview with Jimmy Fallon during an appearance on *The Tonight Show Starring Jimmy Fallon*, posted by "The Tonight Show Starring Jimmy Fallon," June 24, 2020, https://www.youtube.com/watch?v=wWk5U9cKkg8.

9. Michelle Obama, *Becoming*, Kindle edition.

10. Cabane, Olivia Fox, *The Charisma Myth: How Anyone Can Master the Art and Science of Personal Magnetism* (New York City: Portfolio, 2013), Kindle edition.

11. Id., Kindle edition.

12. Diviney, Rich, *The Attributes: 25 Hidden Drivers of Optimal Performance* (New York City: Random House, 2021), Kindle edition.

13. Id.

CHAPTER 7

1. Goldsmith, Marshall, "Answer This Question Before You Commit," LinkedIn newsletter, August 18, 2020, https://www.linkedin.com/pulse/answer-question-before-you-commit-marshall-goldsmith/.

2. Goldsmith, Marshall, interview with Ryan Hawk, *The Learning Leader Show*, "Episode 131: Marshall Goldsmith—The #1 Leadership & CEO Coach in the World," podcast audio, June 8, 2016, https://learningleader .com/episode-131-marshall-goldsmith-the-1-leadership-ceo-coach-in-the -world/.

3. Sondheim, Stephen, "Cinderella at the Grave," *Into the Woods*, lyrics from musical posted at karaoke-lyrics.net, https://www.karaoke-lyrics.net /lyrics/sondheim-stephen/cinderella-at-the-grave-541584.

4. Bohannon, Liz Forkin, interview with Ryan Hawk, *The Learning Leader Show*, "Episode #340: Liz Forkin Bohannon—How to Build Your Life of Purpose, Passion, & Impact (Beginner's Pluck)," podcast audio, November 23, 2019, https://learningleader.com/bohannonhawk340/.

5. Kao, Wes, "Develop Adjacent Skills to Become a Better Operator," blog post, undated, accessed March 26, 2021, https://www.weskao.com/blog /to-become-a-better-marketer-study-these-non-marketing-topics.

6. Collins, Jim, interview with Ryan Hawk, *The Learning Leader Show*, "Episode #398: Jim Collins—The Art of Getting People to Want to Do What Must Be Done (Part 2)," podcast audio, December 20, 2020, https:// learningleader.com/jimcollins398/.

7. "Anne M. Mulcahy," Connecticut Women's Hall of Fame website entry, accessed March 26, 2021, https://www.cwhf.org/inductees/anne -m-mulcahy.

8. Kim, Dustyn, interview with Ryan Hawk, *The Learning Leader Show*, "Episode #410: Dustyn Kim—How to Stand Out & Speak Up (Chief Revenue Officer of Artsy)," podcast audio, March 14, 2021, https://learningleader .com/dustynkim/.

9. Smith, Jodi, "Dave Chappelle Is Low Key Running an A-List Comedy Club in Ohio," Pajiba.com, July 20, 2020, https://www.pajiba.com/celebrities _are_better_than_you/dave-chappelle-is-low-key-running-an-alist -comedy-club-in-yellow-springs-ohio.php.

10. Seinfeld, Jerry, interview with Oliver Burkeman, "Jerry Seinfeld on How to Be Funny Without Sex and Swearing," *The Guardian*, January 5, 2014, https://www.theguardian.com/culture/2014/jan/05/jerry-seinfeld-funny -sex-swearing-sitcom-comedy.

11. Champagne, Christine, "Too Far, or Not Far Enough: How Anthony Jeselnik Writes and Tests His Non-PC Standup Material," *Fast Company*, October 16, 2015, https://www.fastcompany.com/3052383/too-far-or-not -far-enough-how-anthony-jeselnik-writes-and-tests-his-non-pc-standup -act.

12. "Understanding the K-T Boundary," Lunar and Planetary Institute, accessed March 26, 2021, https://www.lpi.usra.edu/science/kring /Chicxulub/. In case you're wondering why the line between the Mesozoic and Cenozoic Eras is referred to as the "K-T Boundary," here's the reason: the last period of time within the Mesozoic Era is known as the Cretaceous Period (from 135 million to 65 million years ago). The first period of the Cenozoic Era is known as the Tertiary Period. *K* is used instead of *C* because the German word for Cretaceous starts with a *K*. As if that weren't confusing enough, there is a move to rename the boundary the *K-Pg boundary* by some geologists who wish to replace the term *Tertiary* with *Paleogene*.

13. "Dinosaurs' Loss Was Frogs' Gain: The Upside of a Mass Extinction," *EurekaAlert!*, July 3, 2017, by the American Association for the Advancement of Science (AAAS), accessed on March 26, 2021, https://www .eurekalert.org/pub_releases/2017-07/uoc--dlw062917.php.

14. Kennedy, Merrit, "How Frogs Benefited from the Dinosaurs' Extinction," *The Two-Way*, blog post, July 3, 2017, https://www.npr.org/sections /thetwo-way/2017/07/03/535383841/how-frogs-benefited-from-the -dinosaurs-extinction.

15. Baker, Lindsay, "Why Embracing Change Is the Key to a Good Life," BBC .com, October 8, 2020, https://www.bbc.com/culture/article/20200930 -why-embracing-change-is-the-key-to-a-good-life.

16. Miller, Donald, interview with Ryan Hawk, *The Learning Leader Show*, "Episode #402: Donald Miller—How to Attract People to Your Mission," podcast audio, January 20, 2021, https://learningleader.com /donaldmiller402/.

17. Id.

18. Wood, Jake, interview with Ryan Hawk, *The Learning Leader Show*, "Episode #391: Jake Wood—How to Accept Risk, Get Candid Feedback, & Love Your Team," podcast audio, November 8, 2020, https://learningleader .com/jakewood391/.

19. Godin, Seth, interview with Ryan Hawk, *The Learning Leader Show*, "Episode #390: Seth Godin—How to Sell Like a Professional, Build Skills, & Ship Creative Work," podcast audio, November 1, 2020, https:// learningleader.com/sethgodin390/.

CHAPTER 8

1. "About > Jeni Britton Bauer," Jenis.com, accessed March 26, 2021, https:// jenis.com/about/about-jeni/.

2. "Henry Crown Classes—Class XXI: 2017," The Aspen Institute's Aspen Global Leadership Network, accessed March 26, 2021, https://agln .aspeninstitute.org/fellowships/henrycrown/classes/XXI.

3. Britton-Bauer, Jeni, interview with Ryan Hawk, *The Learning Leader Show*, "Episode #353: Jeni Britton-Bauer—How to Create a 'Craveable' Reason to Return," podcast audio, February 23, 2020, https://learningleader.com /brittonbauerhawk353/.

4. Collins, Jim, interview with Ryan Hawk, *The Learning Leader Show*, "Episode #397: Jim Collins—How to Create a Generosity Flywheel, Make the Trust Wager, & Earn WHO Luck (Part 1)," podcast audio, December 20, 2020, https://learningleader.com/jimcollins397/.

5. "About me," accessed March 26, 2021, edlatimore.com, https://edlatimore .com/about/.

6. Latimore, Ed, interview with Ryan Hawk, *The Learning Leader Show*, "Episode #389: Ed Latimore—How to Control Your Mind, Body, & Emotions," podcast audio, October 25, 2020, https://learningleader.com /edlatimore389/.

7. Collins, *The Learning Leader Show* Episode #397.

8. Minchin, Tim, "9 Life Lessons—Tim Minchin UWA Address," YouTube video, 18:16, posted by "The University of Western Australia," October 7, 2013, https://www.youtube.com/watch?v=yoEezZD71sc.

9. Beshore, Brent, interview with Ryan Hawk, *The Learning Leader Show*, "Episode #293: Brent Beshore—How to Get Rich Slow & Live an Optimal Life," podcast audio, January 12, 2019, https://learningleader.com /beshorehawk/.

10. "Brent Beshore—CEO/Founder," PermanentEquity.com, accessed March 26, 2021, https://www.permanentequity.com/brent-beshore.

11. *Merriam-Webster Online*, s.v. "credibility," accessed March 26, 2021, https://www.merriam-webster.com/dictionary/credibility.

12. McCroskey, James C., and Jason J. Teven, "Goodwill: A Reexamination of the Construct and Its Measurement," *Communication Monographs* 66, March 1999, http://www.jamescmccroskey.com/publications/180.pdf.

13. Gordon, Jon, interview with Ryan Hawk, *The Learning Leader Show*, "Episode 072: Jon Gordon—Optimistic People Win More | The Energy Bus," podcast audio, November 16, 2015, https://learningleader.com/episode -072-jon-gordon-optimistic-people-win-more-the-energy-bus/.

14. McKay, Brett & Kate, "A Man Is Punctual: The Importance of Being on Time," artofmanliness.com blog post, last updated September 30, 2020, https://www.artofmanliness.com/articles/importance-of-punctuality/.

15. "Junto" is from the Spanish word *junta*, meaning assembly.

16. Franklin, Benjamin, *The Life of Benjamin Franklin: An Autographical Manuscript*, unpublished work made available online by the University of Virginia Library, accessed March 26, 2021, https://anthologydev.lib .virginia.edu/work/Franklin/franklin-autobiography.

17. Holiday, Ryan, interview with Ryan Hawk, *The Learning Leader Show*, "Episode #385: Ryan Holiday—The Art of Living Like a Stoic," podcast audio, September 27, 2020, https://learningleader.com/holidayhawk385/.

18. Babbitt, Frank Cole, *Plutarch's Moralia* (United Kingdom: Harvard University Press, 1949), 241.

CHAPTER 9

1. In 2019, the Michelin Guide removed Sukiyabashi Jiro from its list of 3-star eateries because "Sukiyabashi Jiro does not accept reservations from the general public, which makes it out of our scope," https://www .grubstreet.com/2019/11/michelin-guide-strips-jiro-ono-of-his-three -michelin-stars.html.

2. Joachim, David S., "Obama's First Order of Business in Tokyo: Sushi from the Master," *New York Times*, April 23, 2014, https://www.nytimes.com /2014/04/24/world/asia/obamas-first-order-of-business-in-tokyo-sushi -from-the-master.html.

3. Kober, Jeff, "Bob Iger, Sushi, and Excellence at Disney," blog post at disneyatwork.com, November 2016, http://disneyatwork.com/2016/11 /bob-iger-sushi-and-excellence-at-disney/.

4. Stillman, Jessica, "3 Career Lessons from Sushi Chef Jiro Ono," *Inc.*, December 2, 2014, https://www.inc.com/jessica-stillman/3-career -lessons-from-sushi-chef-jiro-ono.html.

5. Bouloubasis, Victoria, "The Japanese Shokunin Spirit Is a Journey Toward Perfection," blog post at somewheresouthtv.com, May 3, 2020, https:// www.somewheresouthtv.com/post/japanese-shokunin-spirit.

6. Ono, Jiro, *Jiro Dreams of Sushi*, directed by David Gelb (New York, NY: Magnolia Pictures, 2011), DVD.

7. Suzuki, Shunryu, and David Chadwick, *Zen Mind, Beginner's Mind* (United States: Shambhala, 2010), 1.

8. Taleb, Nassim Nicholas, *Fooled by Randomness: The Hidden Role of Chance in Life and in the Markets* (New York: Random House Trade Paperbacks, 2005), Kindle edition.

9. Redick, JJ, interview with Ryan Hawk, *The Learning Leader Show*, "Episode 217: JJ Redick—'You've Never Arrived. You're Always Becoming,'" podcast audio, August 6, 2017, https://learningleader.com/episode-217-jj -redick-youve-never-arrived-youre-always-becoming/.

10. Smith, Mark. "Peter Senge and the Learning Organization," infed.org, April 4, 2013, https://infed.org/mobi/peter-senge-and-the-learning-organization.

11. Milkis, Sidney, "Theodore Roosevelt: Domestic Affairs," millercenter.org, accessed March 26, 2021, https://millercenter.org/president/roosevelt/domestic-affairs.

12. "Richard P. Feynman: Facts," nobelprize.org, accessed March 26, 2021, https://www.nobelprize.org/prizes/physics/1965/feynman/facts/.

13. Gates, Bill. "The Best Teacher I Never Had," YouTube video, 2:36, posted by "Bill Gates" on January 27, 2016, https://www.youtube.com/watch?v=WOoJh6oYAXE.

14. "Project Tuva: Richard Feynman's Messenger Lecture Series," established by Microsoft.com on July 13, 2009, https://www.microsoft.com/en-us/research/project/tuva-richard-feynman/.

15. Evernote, "Learning from the Feynman Technique," August 4, 2017, https://medium.com/taking-note/learning-from-the-feynman-technique-5373014ad230.

16. Rich, Nathanial, "The Novel That Asks, 'What Went Wrong with Mankind?'," *Atlantic*, June 2018, https://www.theatlantic.com/magazine/archive/2018/06/richard-powers-the-overstory/559106/.

17. *Gardner-Webb Basketball 2013-2014 Season Prospectus*, 8, digital version, accessed March 26, 2021, https://issuu.com/marcrabbgwu/docs/prospectus-brief-mbk.

18. *Garner-Webb Basketball 2011-12 Media Guide*, 26, digital version, accessed March 26, 2021, https://issuu.com/marcrabbgwu/docs/hoopsguide12.

19. "Demographic Information," Town of Boiling Springs, NC, website, accessed March 26, 2021, https://www.boilingspringsnc.net/209/Demographic-Information.

20. "List of Big South Coach of the Year Winners," *Coaches Database*, accessed March 26, 2021, https://www.coachesdatabase.com/big-south-coach-of-the-year/.

21. *Gardner-Webb Basketball 2010-11 Media Guide*, 24, digital version, accessed March 26, 2021, https://issuu.com/marcrabbgwu/docs/hoopsguide11.

22. Holtmann, Chris, interview with Ryan Hawk, *The Learning Leader Show*, "Episode #393: Chris Holtmann—How to Lead with Conviction (Don't Be Afraid to Pursue Growth)," podcast audio, November 22, 2020, https://learningleader.com/chrisholtmann393/.

23. Palladino, Paul, "Butler Coach Brandon Miller Takes Leave of Absence for Medical Reasons," SI.com, October 2, 2014, https://www.si.com/college /2014/10/02/butler-coach-brandon-miller-leave-absence.

24. Kniffin, Kevin M., Brian Wansink, Carol M. Devine, and Jeffery Sobal, "Eating Together at the Firehouse: How Workplace Commensality Relates to the Performance of Firefighters," *Human Performance* 28, no.4 (2015): 281–306, https://www.tandfonline.com/doi/full/10.1080/08959285.2015 .1021049.

25. *Merriam-Webster Dictionary Online*, s.v. "commensality," accessed March 26, 2021, https://www.merriam-webster.com/dictionary/commensality.

26. Holmes, Baxter, "Michelin Restaurants and Fabulous Wines: Inside the Secret Team Dinners That Have Built the Spurs' Dynasty," ESPN.com, July 25, 2020, https://www.espn.com/nba/story/_/id/26524600/secret-team -dinners-built-spurs-dynasty.

27. Id.

28. Latimore, *The Learning Leader Show*, Episode #389.

29. Housel, Morgan, interview with Ryan Hawk, *The Learning Leader Show*, "Episode #382: Morgan Housel—Timeless Lessons on Wealth, Greed, & Happiness," podcast audio, September 6, 2020, https://learningleader.com /houselhawk382/.

30. Hardy, Darren, *The Compound Effect: Jumpstart Your Income, Your Life, Your Success* (New York: Hatchette Go, 2020), Kindle edition.

CONCLUSION

1. Roosevelt, Theodore, "Citizenship in a Republic," delivered at the Sorbonne in Paris, France, on April 23, 1910, http://www.worldfuturefund .org/Documents/maninarena.htm.

2. Brown, Brené, *Dare to Lead: Brave Work. Tough Conversations. Whole Hearts* (New York: Random House, 2018), Kindle edition.

3. Robinson, Brandon, "CBS Sports' Clark Kellogg Says President Obama 'Took Advantage' of Him in a 2010 Basketball Game," basketballsocietyonline.com, April 2, 2018, https://basketballsocietyonline .com/clark-kellogg-president-obama-basketball-game.

4. Kellogg, Clark, interview with Ryan Hawk, *The Learning Leader Show*, "Episode #318: Clark Kellogg—How to Take Control of Your Personal Development," podcast audio, July 7, 2019, https://learningleader.com /kellogghawk318/.

5. Waddoups, C. Jeffrey, "Did Employers in the United States Back Away from Skills Training During the Early 2000s?," *ILR Review* 69, no. 2

(March 2016): 405–434, https://journals.sagepub.com/doi/abs/10.1177/0019793915619904.

6. Greene, Robert, interview with Ryan Hawk, *The Learning Leader Show*, "Episode #288: Robert Greene (Part 2)—The Laws of Human Nature," podcast audio, December 12, 2018, https://learningleader.com/robertgreeneryanhawkpart2/.

7. Hinkie, Sam, interview with Patrick O'Shaughnessy, *Invest Like the Best*, "Find Your People," podcast audio, December 15, 2020, transcript, https://www.joincolossus.com/episodes/78487046/hinkie-find-your-people.

8. Id.

9. DuBose, Ben, "Meet Rafael Stone and Eli Witus, the Rockets' New Top Executives," *RocketsWire*, October 15, 2020, https://rocketswire.usatoday.com/2020/10/15/meet-rafael-stone-and-eli-witus-the-rockets-new-top-executives/.

10. "History of the Study," adultdevelopmentstudy.org, accessed March 27, 2021, https://www.adultdevelopmentstudy.org/grantandglueckstudy.

11. Waldinger, Robert "What Makes a Good Life? Lessons from the Longest Study on Happiness," filmed November 2015, TEDxBeaconStreet video, 12:38, https://www.ted.com/talks/robert_waldinger_what_makes_a_good_life_lessons_from_the_longest_study_on_happiness?language=en.

12. Galloway, Scott, interview with Ryan Hawk, *The Learning Leader Show*, "Episode #396: Scott Galloway—Making Predictions, Sharing Love, & Turning Crisis to Opportunity," podcast audio, December 13, 2020, https://learningleader.com/scottgalloway396/.

13. Chappelle, Dave, "Dave Chappelle Acceptance Speech | 2019 Mark Twain Prize," YouTube video, 8:23, filmed October 27, 2019, posted by "Beyond Time News," January 10, 2020, https://www.youtube.com/watch?v=aeYA72NLaDE.

INDEX

ABOUT THE AUTHOR

Ryan Hawk is the creator and host of *The Learning Leader Show*, a top-rated business podcast that focuses on learning from the smartest, most thoughtful leaders in the world. He has interviewed over 450 leaders, including such luminaries as Simon Sinek, Seth Godin, Kat Cole, General Stanley McChrystal, Jim Collins, and Adam Grant. *The Learning Leader Show* has listeners in 156 countries. *Forbes* called it "the most dynamic leadership podcast out there," and *Inc.* magazine listed the show as one of the top five podcasts to "help you lead smarter." Ryan is the author of *Welcome to Management: How to Grow from Top Performer to Excellent Leader*, which Forbes called "the best leadership book of 2020."

A sought-after professional speaker, Ryan also serves as a leadership advisor with Insight Global, a leader in the staffing industry known for its incredible culture. He writes the email newsletter *Mindful Monday* with tens of thousands of readers, and conducts Leadership Circles with leaders from Fortune 50 companies, entrepreneurs, professional athletes, and coaches. Previously, he was a sales professional for 12 years at LexisNexis and Elsevier. He worked his way up from entry level to Vice President of North American Sales.

For more information, please visit LearningLeader.com.

Because learning changes everything.®

"Every new manager makes mistakes. But you might make fewer of them if you follow the practical advice that Ryan Hawk has spent years collecting."

—Adam Grant, *New York Times* bestselling author of *Think Again* and host of the TED podcast *WorkLife*